# Insiders' Guide to Technology-Assisted Review (TAR)

T0288027

# Insiders' Guide to Technology-Assisted Review (TAR)

**ERNST & YOUNG LLP**

WILEY

For general information on our other products and services or for technical support, please contact our Customer Care Department within the United States at (800) 762-2974, outside the United States at (317) 572-3993 or fax (317) 572-4002.

Wiley publishes in a variety of print and electronic formats and by print-on-demand. Some material included with standard print versions of this book may not be included in e-books or in print-on-demand. If this book refers to media such as a CD or DVD that is not included in the version you purchased, you may download this material at http://booksupport.wiley.com. For more information about Wiley products, visit www.wiley.com.

*Library of Congress Cataloging-in-Publication Data:*

ISBN 978-1-118-89426-2 (Paperback)
ISBN 978-1-118-894323 (ePDF)
ISBN 978-1-118-89438-5 (ePub)

Printed in the United States of America

10 9 8 7 6 5 4 3 2 1

# Contents

# Preface

For many years, courts and lawmakers have been struggling with the challenges that ever increasing volumes of data pose to the legal process. Exponentially increasing digital information is hardly a phenomenon that took us by surprise. In litigation and internal and regulatory investigations, as well as information management more broadly, it is largely corporate parties who are footing the bills.

Where finding the truth requires making sense of information and when there is so much of it, we need new tools that will help us to rise above the mostly irrelevant oceans of potentially discoverable information. Technology-Assisted Review, a potentially broad term that has been used to reference any use of technology that facilitates document review as part of the discovery process, has more recently been used (especially in its abbreviated form "TAR") in a narrower sense related to predictive coding and various forms of review-enhancing analytics. In all of its various forms, TAR holds real promise for alleviating the problems associated with performing accurate searches of large volumes of data from a multitude of sources.

This book explores the linguistic and technical issues associated with the use of TAR in the legal context, as well as summarizing the small body of case law that has percolated over predictive coding. The introduction provides the historical background of TAR in terms of its evolution in support of litigations and investigations. In Chapter 1, we describe different structures of document review, which we look at as a form of classification in which individual items are labeled according to criteria provided by a set of requests, such as in a discovery document request.

A small but growing body of case law on predictive coding, which often explicitly references "thought leadership" publications as quasi-authoritative, is discussed in Chapter 2. Reflecting the broader trend in electronic discovery, legal principles applied to predictive coding include transparency, proportionality, and defensibility, with a heavy dose of recommended cooperation between opposing parties. Appropriate degrees of transparency into an adversary's discovery process and the appropriate balance between cooperation and advocacy are still very much in dispute.

Chapter 3 explores the economics of TAR in terms of cost and value.

This book represents an attempt to provide professionals without advanced degrees in statistics, linguistics, or machine learning and the related technology of TAR a resource for obtaining a thorough understanding of the theory and practice of TAR. Given the rapidly increasing importance of TAR to the legal process, such an understanding is indispensable to legal professionals and others faced with the problem of making sense of large document collections. While the technology of TAR will undoubtedly continue to advance at a speed that makes it hard to capture in writing, the underlying concepts will hold true. The purpose of this book is to convey an understanding of those concepts to the practitioner.

# Introduction—
# Evolution of TAR

The evolutionary path of modern Technology-Assisted Review (TAR) was paved as much by necessity as it was by innovation. These advanced solutions are now necessary because traditional review workflows simply cannot keep pace with the growing volume of electronically stored information (ESI). Moreover, heightened awareness of the potential flaws associated with linear review[1] has called unwanted attention to the very real potential for inaccurate coding and incomplete productions.

At the same time, the underlying discipline that drives TAR methodology—the art and science of information retrieval (IR)—has been widely accepted in government and industry-specific sectors (accounting, finance, insurance, tele-communications, and health care to name a few). This active and ongoing use of IR methodology to search, mine, and manage large sets of electronic data has allowed these innovative solutions to go through decades of testing and validation before reaching the mainstream legal marketplace. And while the use of technology is not new or novel in the discovery arena, the road to modern TAR has been paved with numerous iterations of technology-assisted workflows.

In the literal sense, "technology-assisted review" has been ongoing since the first computer was used to help log or categorize a set of documents in response to a request for production. Database capabilities and sophistication grew rapidly during this inaugural wave of technology-assisted solutions, allowing for document collections and productions to be tracked through delimited fields and warehoused indefinitely.

Further advancements came with the ability to scan the physical image of each document and render that image as a static file in a separate database that could be accessed on demand by reviewers through network connections. Combined with what was then considered a cutting-edge technology called optical character recognition (OCR), reviewers could access search results for both the image of a document and its underlying text in one location. Technology-assisted review was in its renaissance and the legal community fully embraced these solutions.

This was the dawn of the digital age in which paper collections were starting to be replaced by word processing tools and the default standard for business

1

correspondence switched from written letters to electronically transmitted e-mails. With this sea change under way, yet another wave of literal "technology-assisted review" solutions was under development: data processing and hosting applications.

Electronic documents must go through a series of highly technical steps before they can be reviewed. The data needs to be collected (without corrupting or spoliating the evidence), standardized to isolate only the user-created files, deduplicated to reduce the cost of reviewing the same document twice, and then rendered for review in a hosted application that presents a genuine version of the original native file for analysis. Breakdowns during any of these steps will result in the loss of important information about the document and the potential that the data will be inadmissible if presented as evidence in a court of law.

One of the greatest advantages of data processing is that we learn a lot about the data set as it is staged for review. The extracted text and metadata for each document contain troves of information that can be used to help organize these files in a meaningful way. That effort can be as simple as grouping the documents by custodian or by search results, or made more complex by introducing some of the early TAR systems such as clustering or ranking the documents based on underlying content. These solutions are the natural progression of performing legal discovery in the digital age and represent the starting point for modern TAR in application.

TAR solutions, in all of the structural varieties outlined in Chapter 1, as well as during their early developmental states described above, still need to be executed through a workflow that involves trained professionals reviewing a collection of documents. Therefore, it is equally important to consider the review process alongside evolving technology to fully understand the evolutionary path.

From the early 1980s to mid-1990s, legal document reviews were fairly straightforward: locate just enough space to accommodate any given set of boxes and the appropriate number of people needed to review the contents, fill the seats with junior lawyers or senior paralegals, and start the project. Reviews were exclusively linear in this time period; the contents of each box would be reviewed from front to back with some color coding or physical marking to identify relevant and/or privileged documents. Little if any thought was given to technology, infrastructure, or workspace ergonomics and only modest consideration was paid to the workforce supporting this effort—reviews were often performed in windowless basements or off-site archive facilities with limited amenities, effectively isolated from the legal case team.

This underscores the fundamental problem with discovery in the digital age: it has become disconnected from the legal process that gave rise to the obligation in the first place. The ultimate goal of discovery is to facilitate a complete and accurate factual record and to put the salient facts on the table so practitioners can advocate for the best interests of their clients based on the merits of the case.

Document review in the new millennium has responded to many of these concerns. Review centers have been moved out of the basement into fully modernized facilities with workspace designed to ensure the security of client data as well as reviewer comfort. Centers are equipped with redundant high-speed internet connections and a dedicated IT staff to support the technology infrastructure that is the backbone of a modern document review. There is an enormous pool of talented and experienced review attorneys with specialized substantive skills to meet the needs of any legal matter. Finally, workflows are being designed and implemented by experienced project managers to ensure that efficiencies are realized and costs are reduced wherever possible.

Despite the many advances in early TAR solutions and document review protocols, the ability to accurately and consistently analyze data is simply not able to keep pace with the proliferation of ESI in today's corporate and social environments. There are simply too many data sources and too much raw data. So how can the legal community feel confident that modern TAR methods are achieving their intended purpose? How can modern TAR reconnect discovery with the merits of the case, reduce cost, and improve quality?

The answer to that lies in the chapters ahead and detailed discussions of the next generation of TAR solutions, increased judicial acceptance, and the application of modern TAR to legal review above and beyond discovery.

## Note

1. See The Sedona Conference, *The Sedona Conference Best Practices Commentary on the Use of Search and Information Retrieval Methods in E-Discovery*, 8 SEDONA CONF. J. 189, 194, 199 (2007); Maura R. Grossman and Gordon V. Cormack, *Technology-Assisted Review in E-Discovery Can Be More Effective and More Efficient Than Exhaustive Manual Review*, XVII RICH. J.L. & TECH. 11 (2011), http://jolt.richmond.edu/v17i3/article11.pdf.

# CHAPTER 1

# TAR: A Structural Analysis

Fueled by advances in computer software and the ready availability of the computer hardware on which it runs, modern technology has made it possible to create and preserve almost unimaginable amounts of digital information. We create this information with technology running over electronic circuits at the speed of light. This information takes many forms: database fields and database entries, formal business documents (contracts, patents, health information, HR records), e-mail correspondence, text messages, e-commerce communications, voice recordings, photographs, video. We interact with this information directly, as producers of electronic documents or as recipients of electronic communication in one of its many guises. And we are often motivated—by interest or obligation—to interact with this digital information in less direct ways. Whether we want to recover information, explore it, extract it, classify it or leverage it, accessing the electronically stored information inevitably involves digital technology. In the simplest case, we depend on digital technology to display information or print it or play it audibly. But there are more complex cases in which we may not have identified how the information we need or want is represented in a document collection, or even whether it is represented in that collection at all.

In the context of electronic discovery, the technological infrastructure supporting interaction with the information represented in electronic data sets can be referred to by the phrase "technology-assisted review." Technology-assisted review in this sense plays a pivotal role in the entire review process: storing, collecting, transferring, processing, hosting, searching, culling, displaying, up to the point of producing identified results. This broad technological infrastructure has evolved through the interaction of legal traditions, standards, and requirements; theoretical and applied information retrieval; the independent development of applicable technologies that are eventually brought in to alleviate the burdens and enhance the quality of discovery; and the market forces that drive innovation and reward success.

Recently, a narrower interpretation of technology-assisted review, abbreviated "TAR," has emerged, one in which it is closely connected with technology that enhances the efficiency or effectiveness of review, and particularly, with the term "predictive coding." Although this narrower sense seems to mean slightly different things to different people, it is applied to technology that significantly automates the core task of review—the classification of documents as relevant or not to one or more specifications. Technologically, this automation or partial automation can be addressed in a variety of ways, each with accompanying advantages and disadvantages. If TAR can be successfully achieved, with standardized methods and appropriate controls, the potential benefits are noteworthy: TAR seems to offer a direct way of confronting exploding growth in volumes, corresponding growth in costs (for traditional methods of linear review), and even possible improvements in the quality of results.

But a clear grasp of the actual situation is hard to attain. There are two main barriers. The first is the presence of many competing technologies, constructed in complex ways from sophisticated assumptions that are often beyond the reach of those who need them most. Second, these complex technologies connect to familiar properties of document review "workflow" in different ways. In fact, the same technological component can play different roles, so that the relation between technology and function is not simple and direct, but many-many.

In spite of these complexities, we believe that the ways in which technology can interact with the core task of review can be expressed in a simple structural breakdown. In what follows, we characterize the structural principles upon which this analysis depends and describe their application and interaction. The result is revealing. Different TAR technologies are compatible with different structures: Some technologies, intrinsically more powerful, are compatible with multiple and distinct structural configurations of document review; others have limited compatibility with structural configurations.

One benefit of this structural view is terminological: the structural choices, which do not depend on terminology, offer a clear meaning to the terms we select to name them (as long as we select these terms with sufficient care). Since all of the structural choices—including linear review—are strongly dependent on technology in one form or another, they are all instances of technology-assisted review in the broad sense. We use the acronym "TAR" to cover a variety of special cases, most importantly, predictive coding and what we call "accelerated review." In our structural analysis, each special case is endowed with its own transparent name.

We use the terminology introduced in the structural as a conceptual framework overview throughout the chapters that follow.

# The Core Task of eDiscovery

An essential problem of eDiscovery is to identify within a universe of potentially responsive documents the subset that is relevant and/or responsive to a specification of some kind, for example Request for Production (RFP), Subpoena, or HSR Second Request. (For purposes of our discussion here, we will use "RFP" to include any such specification.) Thus, we have two basic models: a model of the documents and a model of the RFP. Review and production depends on both models. In general, review does not depend only on the document collection; it depends equally on the RFP. (For example, a single document collection can be the source of documents satisfying distinct and incompatible requests. This would be impossible if review results were dependent solely on document properties and not on requests.) Not surprisingly, then, the way in which the document model and the RFP model are brought into contact in review structurally illuminates many intuitive and familiar distinctions in the review landscape.

## 1.1 Linear Review

We define "linear review" to mean a review in which every labeled document in the reviewable universe is individually labeled as relevant/nonrelevant by a human reviewer. In contrast, in a nonlinear review, there is at least one labeled document in the reviewable universe that is not individually labeled as relevant/nonrelevant by a human reviewer. We use the term "TAR" to refer to any form of nonlinear review. Valuable TAR systems will apply document labeling to many documents, but we can draw a principled line at one. We can represent the structure of review thus far as a simple split between TAR and linear review. (See Figure 1.1.)

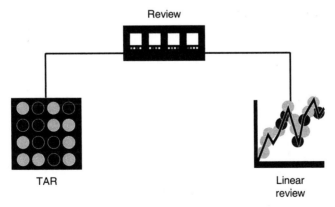

**FIGURE 1.1** TAR Branches Separately from Linear Review

## 1.2 TAR

In a TAR system, not every label on every document is supplied by human reviewers: Combining the interpretation of the RFP with the experience of a document set is to be replaced by automated steps in some way. But how? We would like to be able to specify all the possibilities or "the solution space" to this problem. From our perspective, there is a simple structural property that bifurcates the solution space.

In some forms of TAR, human reviewers don't label all documents individually, but all labels are applied by human reviewers. The technological leverage in this case involves relations among documents (especially, relations of similarity of some kind, as found in clustering), rather than relations involving both documents and requests. We call this form of TAR "accelerated review."

In the remaining forms of TAR, labels are applied to documents in a way that doesn't depend directly on human review.

Typically, the document set is provisionally classified into labeled subsets that correspond to the parts of the RFP; the provisional hypothesis is tested (by sampling) and, if deemed necessary, tuned and improved. We call this form of TAR "predictive coding." (See Figure 1.2.)

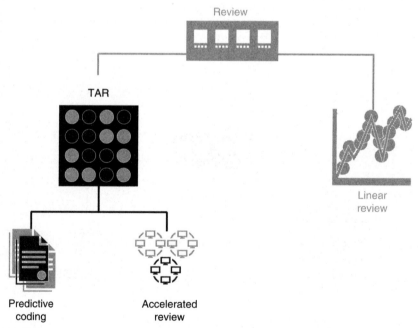

**FIGURE 1.2**   Predictive Coding and Accelerated Review Are Two Different Branches of TAR

## 1.2.1 Accelerated Review

As noted above, one way to cut down the number of "touches" in document labeling (for purposes of reducing cost and increasing accuracy), while still relying on human review as the labeling mechanism, is to label sets of documents rather than each of the individual documents contained in these sets. There are many ways to cluster similar documents together so that if documents are sufficiently similar in some respect, they may belong to the same cluster in a set of many clusters. It is the user's expectation—or hope—that documents belonging to the same cluster will have other properties in common—properties like responsiveness or relevance.

Approaches to clustering involve, among other things, different measures of similarity or dissimilarity and different goals in grouping. A few basic points about the role of clustering in review are:

- Clustering doesn't necessarily entail that documents in the same cluster are label-equivalent: A perfectly sound method of clustering is to assign documents that have the same number of occurrences of certain words in their contents, but it is unlikely that this method alone will produce label-equivalent clusters (i.e., that all of the documents in a cluster are relevant or not relevant).
- Clustering should not be dominated by boilerplate or irrelevant material such as signature lines, footers, embedded messages, etc.
- If bulk coding is based on statistical sampling, the protocol should be described and adhered to; if it isn't based on statistical sampling, what is it based on?
- The bulk coding protocol should characterize the criteria by which a cluster is associated with a label, as well as the procedure to be followed when no label can be consistently applied to the members of a cluster.

In the form of clustering that we have described, the key characteristic is that every cluster is labeled by human review. But if a label assigned to a cluster propagates automatically to each member of the cluster, regardless of whether that member has been individually reviewed, this is not linear review, but a form of TAR.

## 1.2.2 Predictive Coding

In accelerated review, technology is applied to make the review process more efficient, but all the labeling that takes place is done by direct human interactions. In contrast, in predictive coding, the labels of the RFP classes are brought actively into the technology: The goal is to predict what label or labels should be associated with each document. In short, technology is used to construct a hypothetical model of the response to the RFP. This can be done in a variety of ways, but they share certain common properties.

**1.2.2.1 MODELS** The goal of a classifier is to associate individual items with appropriate classes. If we think of human document review as a form of classification, the reviewer is the classifier, an individual item is a document, and there are (in the simplest case) two classes: responsive and nonresponsive. A simple model of this situation is a labeling of documents as belonging to one class or the other (but not both). If we would like to assess how good our model is, we can compare the labeling produced by our original reviewer to the labeling produced by our model on the same set of documents. Such a comparison must deal with four possible cases:

- Reviewer labels document d as responsive; model labels d responsive.
- Reviewer labels document d as nonresponsive; model labels d nonresponsive.
- Reviewer labels document d as responsive; model labels d nonresponsive.
- Reviewer labels document d as nonresponsive; model labels d responsive.

It's often useful to summarize a comparison of this kind in the form of a table, where we represent the point of view of the reviewer in the columns and the point of view of the model in the rows. (See Figure 1.3.)

Just as we have four cases above—two ways for reviewer and model to agree and two ways to disagree—we have four cells in the table. We've labeled the cells with standard terminology, assuming that the reviewer's classification is true and the model is attempting to conform to the reviewer. (The other perspective is also possible: imagine training a person to classify items by example.) If we populate the cells with numbers generated by an actual comparison, we can use them to calculate such standard metrics as precision (the ratio of true positives to model-labeled reponsives (true positives + false positives) and recall (the ratio of true positives to reviewer-labeled responsives (true positives + false negatives).

What makes this a simple model is the fact that all we care about is which of the four possible cases the compared labeling of a particular document by two classifiers (here the reviewer and the model) falls into. In this kind of model comparison, nothing else matters.

But not all models are simple, and in richer models, other things do matter. For example, suppose we try to model the reviewer, not just the review results. The reviewer absorbs the information from the RFP and the informational properties of each document, and uses these informational sources to decide whether the document is responsive to the RFP or not.

To model this situation, we might focus on two phases: the training phase (in which the reviewer masters the RFP information, perhaps using some initial interaction with a sample of documents) and the decision phase (in which the trained reviewer classifies documents not previously encountered as responsive to the RFP or not). Since the reviewer and the model of the reviewer both provide simple models consisting of labeled document lists, we can still measure the performance of our more complex model by comparing these two simple models as discussed above.

| Model label | Reviewer label | |
|---|---|---|
| | Responsive | Nonresponsive |
| Responsive | True Positive | False Positive |
| Nonresponsive | False Negative | True Negative |

**FIGURE 1.3**  Comparing Reviewer Labels with Model Labels

In machine-learning approaches, a statistical algorithm is trained on the correlation of document features and review labeling on a subset of the reviewable universe. It then projects (or generalizes) this correlation to the universe as a whole. From the point of view of modeling, there are two simple models: the partial model based on review of a sample of the data and the projected model over the universe as a whole. These two simple models must have a more abstract common basis, richer and more complexly structured than a collection of lists.

Another approach is to specify the response to an RFP as the response to a query (perhaps a query based on an ontology—a relational network over words and concepts). On this approach, the query plays the role of the partial model that is projected over the universe as a whole. A major difference with the machine-learning approach is that the query approach is usually constructed manually, through iterative trial-and-error interaction with the data.

Accordingly, we extend our structural model of predictive coding and review by splitting it into two subparts—machine-learning classification and manual classification. (See Figure 1.4.) In the first, the RFP information is brought into contact

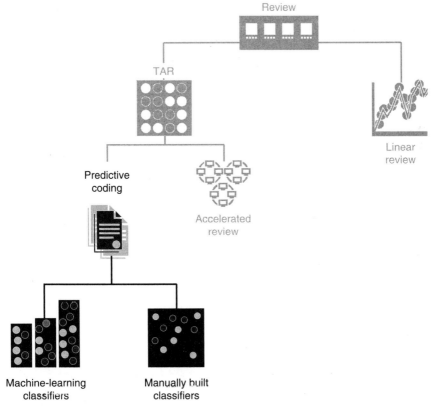

**FIGURE 1.4** Machine-Learning and Manually Built Classifiers Are Two Different Branches of Predictive Coding

with the document collection by reviewers who label a sample of the document collection; the labeled sample is then used to train (and test) the machine-learning components. In the second, the RFP information is brought into contact with the document collection by the team building the classifier. As we will see later, both systems typically take advantage of iterative training, tuning, and improvement.

## 1.3 Hybrid Systems

Although the structural differentiation between the types of review represented in the diagram above are clear in principle, in practice, distinct forms of review are often mixed: There are frequently good reasons why different subpopulations of the review universe may be treated differently.

One common example is the use of predictive coding to identify and segregate various classes of nonrelevant documents, in a way that speeds up the review of the remainder of documents. Thus, this combination uses partial predictive coding to achieve the goals of accelerated review.

Another prominent example is ranked retrieval, in which the review universe is ranked (ideally, at least) from most probably relevant to least probably relevant. This ranking offers a natural way to prioritize review: Start at the top with the most probable and work down until a determination is made that a level of not probable enough to continue has been reached. This is a useful place to stop review. And stopping can be further justified by sampling the remainder.

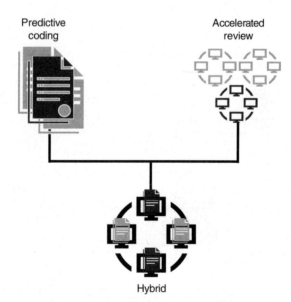

**FIGURE 1.5**   Hybrid Review Is a Combination of Predictive Coding and Accelerated Review

Since hybrid systems like these are prevalent in practice, they deserve a place in our structural diagram. The clearest way to do this is to hide the distinction between the subtypes of predictive coding, to add a node "hybrid," and to link it to Predictive Coding and Accelerated Review. (See Figure 1.5.)

## 1.4 Summary

In this structural analysis of the forms of TAR, we have used structural principles to draw principled distinctions among a variety of technology-enhanced forms of review. These structural principles are based on how the information contained in an RFP is brought into contact with individual documents or sets of documents to determine relevance.

In the pure form of linear review, every document is individually reviewed, so that the connecting point of RFP-information and document properties is located in each individual labeling of each document by a reviewer.

TAR is simply nonlinear review: one or more documents (usually many more) are labeled without being individually labeled by a human reviewer.

In accelerated review, all labels are still applied by human reviewers, but not all documents are labeled individually. The paradigm case of accelerated review is clustering of documents according to some measure of similarity or dissimilarity, with the expectation (or hope) that documents that are similar according to this measure are also similar in relation to the RFP categories (plus the nonrelevant category defined as none of the RFP categories).

Predictive coding uses document properties and RFP information to construct a measurable model of the response by the review universe to the RFP. A basic distinction within predictive coding is whether the model is built with machine-learning methods or manually, using human intelligence and tradecraft. In either case, predictive coding models can be iteratively trained and tested. Their quality can be quantitatively measured using standard statistical techniques.

# CHAPTER 2

# TAR and The Case Law

## 2.1 Introduction

TAR is part of the fabric of electronic discovery. It represents a natural part of the movement toward making discovery possible without cataclysmic economic consequences and the toppling of a legal system based on the search for the truth. Without TAR, the scope of legal discovery would either have to narrow dramatically or parties would find themselves unable to comply with discovery obligations for lack of money and time. Even with TAR, fundamental views of discovery have been forever altered as a result of ever-increasing data volume, variety and velocity, or "Big Data."[1] Principles such as proportionality, transparency, and even cooperation are widely (although not universally) viewed as essential if electronic discovery is to continue to be part of our legal system. TAR is well suited to adhere to these principles.

There are published opinions where the use of TAR has been the subject of discovery disputes, and there are cases where courts have "recommended" to parties that they use TAR to relieve burdensome electronic discovery obligations. However, there is still little in the way of published law directly addressing TAR (and nothing in the way of authoritative precedent), despite the bellwether, high drama of *Moore v. Publicis Groupe, et. al.*,[2] discussed below. Nevertheless, it is possible to make educated guesses about where the trend is heading in terms of court attitudes toward TAR, not only through interpretation of case law but also through thought leadership publications and dialogue at conferences and in other continuing legal education settings. The trend is undeniably toward promoting greater use.

As a sign of the times, consider the comment submitted by the Duke University School of Law Center for Judicial Studies, dated October 17, 2013. In response to the proposed amendments to the Federal Rules of Civil Procedure published for public comment on August 15, 2013, by the Civil Rules Advisory Committee, it proposed that the following sentence be added to the committee note to Rule 26(b)(1):

> *As part of the proportionality considerations, parties are encouraged, in appropriate cases, to consider the use of advanced analytical software applications and other technologies that can screen for relevant and privileged documents in ways that are at least as accurate as manual review, at far less cost.*

One of the great debates in electronic discovery with particular relevance to TAR is about the extent to which producing parties should be required to disclose the methods, as well as technologies, that underpin their productions. Differing approaches to such disclosure are taken to some degree by Magistrate Judge Peck in *Moore* and Magistrate Judge Nolan in *Kleen Products*.[3] On one side of this debate are those who argue that this kind of transparency has never been required in the past, so there is no reason the use of TAR should change the existing paradigm. They point out that, historically, requesting parties were not routinely allowed to inquire into a producing party's document selection methods or criteria unless they could show that there was some kind of defect in the production. Even then, the inquiry would be limited to the particular defects shown, as opposed to a general inquiry into how documents were identified for production. It is arguable that a certain degree of opacity is justified because inquiring past a certain point would reveal the attorney's thought process, which is a classic "work product" that is protected from production.

The opposing view holds that electronic discovery has changed these dynamics. Given the amount of filtering that necessarily takes place between an original universe of documents and what is ultimately produced, as well as the complexities involved in performing all manner of legally necessary operations on ESI, from preservation through production, huge gaps in production could arise from small decisions, computational errors, misconfigurations of technology, search terms, etc. Clearly, TAR adds additional opportunities for divergence and disagreement. Moreover, holders of this view argue that they just want to know what was done—a factual matter—as opposed to why it was done.

There is little question that opponents of transparency appear to have an uphill struggle. This was clear with the amendments to the Federal Rules of Civil Procedure enacted in 2006. Rule 26(f) was modified to require that the "meet and confer" include a discussion of electronic discovery issues. While there was no specific direction as to what (or even whether) parties need to discuss how they arrived at their document production, the clear mandate is that greater cooperation and transparency is a necessity if electronic discovery is not going to hopelessly bog down an important element of our legal system. The proper application of this mandate to TAR, however, is the subject of debate.

The idea behind requiring more up-front discussion about electronic discovery is to prevent disagreements from derailing the process and delaying adjudication of the issues. Given the effort and expenditure involved in obtaining and migrating ESI from preservation through production, finding out after the fact that the entire effort will need to be done differently would be, to put it mildly, inefficient. As demonstrated in some of the cases discussed below, the idea that a party should redo a major production effort because there was purportedly a more accurate way of doing things, or because there was a flaw in the specific TAR process, raises the hackles of those involved in the process—or even more, of those who pay for it. Rule 26(f) shows that courts expect parties to discuss what they need to in advance to avoid situations where many miles down the litigation road, and millions of client dollars later, they discover there was a wrong turn and the steps must be retraced.

Notwithstanding the amendment, a constant refrain has been heard from the judiciary that parties are not adhering to the new rule and instead are still conducting "drive-by" 26(f) conferrals. In other words, lawyers are not adequately addressing the electronic discovery issues that could grind the case to a halt later. An increasing number of opinions chastise parties for failing to raise electronic discovery issues at the meet and confer stage and refuse to grant relief because of this failure.[4] The upshot is that an ill-considered decision to avoid transparency early in a matter comes at the risk of eventually getting stuck somewhere unpleasant (and expensive) to remedy the problems that result.

The electronic discovery processes used by parties are too frequently subject to discovery themselves to insist that the old ways of doing things should persist. The train has left the station. Electronic discovery processes should not be something you are ashamed of or afraid to show your adversary. Chances are you will have to do so sooner or later, either as attorney work product or in a theoretical debate over the most appropriate approach.

With respect to TAR in the broad sense, many opinions in recent years show a judicial expectation of open discussion of and attempt to find agreement on search terms.[5] At a minimum, the notion that electronic keyword search terms used to find responsive documents should be protected as work product may be fading fast. Generally, this level of disclosure of the document selection and review process has become a routine and expected part of electronic discovery procedure in many quarters, although opponents of such transparency are still mounting vigorous defenses when it comes to specific aspects of TAR, for example, "seed sets."

And then there is the Sedona Conference's "Cooperation Proclamation."[6] This document, weighty by virtue of the many judicial signatures it has attracted, mandates that all lawyers should just try to get along when it comes to electronic discovery. Lawyers who resist sharing their electronic discovery processes risk being branded uncooperative, and no prudent lawyer wants a judge to think they are uncooperative. Cases described below (as well as others) have cited this proclamation, and any debate about whether cooperation is consistent with the lawyer's duty to be a zealous, vigorous, or otherwise enthusiastic advocate for the client is merely academic. The finer distinctions about what level of disclosures in the spirit of cooperation are consistent with the adversarial system can be argued, but the appearance of noncooperation will not help anyone get the TAR solution they want.

## 2.2 Emerging Case Law

### 2.2.1 Judicial Recognition of TAR—*Moore*[7]

While discussion of TAR in the electronic discovery "community" started in earnest long before (actually, many years before) it appeared in any judicial opinion, the proverbial stake in the ground was driven by a Magistrate Judge in federal court in New York. This judge was known for his active involvement in electronic discovery, through his judicial opinions and through participation in thought leadership conferences and publications (a factor that became a subject of contention in the case discussed below). *Moore* involved gender and pregnancy discrimination claims against large advertising companies. In *Moore*, Magistrate Judge Andrew Peck of the U.S. District Court for the Southern District of New York unambiguously held that there is no *a priori* reason that the use of TAR should be barred in litigation. In other words, TAR is an acceptable tool for compliance with electronic discovery obligations given the right conditions and circumstances, or as Judge Peck put it: "This judicial opinion now recognizes that computer-assisted review is an acceptable way to search for relevant ESI in appropriate cases."[8]

It is questionable as to whether this statement should be surprising to anyone. It's more of a "someone finally said what everyone else was thinking" situation. Did anyone ever suggest that TAR is acceptable in inappropriate cases or unacceptable in appropriate cases? Perhaps not in so many words, but the idea that traditional means of relying on manual, linear review aided by keyword searching could be replaced by more automated means—and with more accurate outcomes—was new to many lawyers. It is easy for professionals steeped in electronic discovery to forget that their knowledge of and attitudes toward the use of TAR are not necessarily representative of the much broader population involved, voluntarily or involuntarily, in legal discovery of ESI.

While certain interested parties sought to make more of this "endorsement" than Judge Peck meant it to be and to tie it to certain products, he was quick to readjust these proclamations: "To correct the many blogs about this case, initiated by a press release from plaintiffs' vendor—the Court did not order the parties to use predictive coding. The parties had agreed to defendants' use of it, but had disputes over the scope and implementation, which the Court ruled on, thus accepting the use of computer-assisted review in this lawsuit."[9] This is actually a murky point in *Moore*, at least to the extent that the plaintiffs consider their alleged assent to the use of predictive coding to be misstated.

During the course of his written opinion, following up on an earlier ruling from the bench, Judge Peck referenced and quoted from his own article on TAR, in which he defines "computer-assisted coding" as "tools . . . that use sophisticated algorithms to enable the computer to determine relevance, based on interaction with (i.e., training by) a human reviewer." He says that TAR involves a "seed set" of documents reviewed and coded by "a senior partner (or [small] team)" and that "[t]he computer identifies properties of those documents that it uses to code other documents." Then "the computer predicts" further coding based on further review by the "senior reviewer." He further states that "[t]ypically, the senior lawyer (or team) needs to review only a few thousand documents to train the computer."[10]

The following discussion provides a glimpse into the ensuing drama around the defendants' proposed protocol and the plaintiffs' vehement objections, as well as Judge Peck's response to those objections. There is a high volume of spilled ink about the predictive coding protocol, as well as plaintiffs' relentless (although ultimately unsuccessful) efforts to seek recusal of Judge Peck. Some of the highlights are included below.

With respect to the "how" of resolving disagreements about the use of predictive coding, a recurring and fundamental question is whether expert testimony is necessary to support proposed technology, methodology, or protocol. Judge Peck says *Daubert* gatekeeping rules for expert testimony do not apply to the search for discoverable information as opposed to the admissibility of the discovered evidence, but nevertheless that process and results are still important. He quotes from his own article: ". . . I will want to know what was done and why that produced defensible results," but "I may be less interested in the science behind the 'black box' of the vendor's software than [in the results]."[11]

However, according to Judge Peck, transparency "would include disclosing the 'seed set' as well as how the 'seed set' documents were coded (but not why)." Defensibility requires that "quality control would have to be demonstrated."[12] Finally, in what has become a refrain from courts writing about TAR, Judge Peck's opinions indicate that no one gets very far in TAR without cooperation consistent with the Sedona Cooperation Proclamation.[13] (The fourth horseman is proportionality.)

The plaintiffs did not agree with Judge Peck's views on whether expert testimony is necessary to support a predictive coding proposal.[14] They cite the *Kleen Products*[15] case, discussed below, to support the notion that Judge Peck should have held an evidentiary hearing with experts to ensure reliability and accuracy of the proposed protocol.[16] They also cite *Victor Stanley Inc. v. Creative Pipe, Inc.*[17]—"resolving contested issues of whether a particular search and information retrieval method was appropriate . . . involves scientific, technical or specialized information."

Judge Peck distinguishes *Kleen Products* from *Moore*. In *Moore*, he asserts that both parties agreed to the use of predictive coding, while the plaintiffs take issue with this characterization. Rather, they view their statements as meaning that they only agreed to consider predictive coding conditionally—*if* they could work out a protocol satisfactory to them. Whether this means they agreed to predictive coding if implemented correctly or that they didn't agree to predictive coding if not implemented correctly is something lawyers could probably argue about until the end of time.

The record in *Moore* reveals much debate regarding the brass tacks of the proposed protocol, though the parties also disagreed about more fundamental discovery issues, including custodians and ESI sources subject to discovery. The plaintiffs had many specific objections to the way the defendants proposed to carry out their computer-assisted review. Some of the elements of the proposed protocol and areas of agreement and disagreement are identified below.[18]

In court conferences and in a lot of lawyerly back and forth, the plaintiffs objected to the defendants' proposal that after the computer was "fully trained" they would review the top 40,000 documents (at an estimated cost of $200,000). Judge Peck described this objection as a "pig in a poke." In his view the right number would be determined by "what the statistics would show for the results."[19] In other words, if the determined number would result in excessively high nonproduction of responsive documents, it couldn't be the correct number.

The parties agreed that a 95% confidence level could be used, plus or minus 2%, as the basis for a random sample that would be used to identify the seed set to "train the predictive coding software." They disagreed on the defendants' review of the random sample *before* the parties had agreed on the addition of two "concept groups" or "issue tags." The defendants proposed that the plaintiffs code the random sample, which the defendant produced, for these issue tags. The defendants would then incorporate these tags. The plaintiffs' vendor assented.[20]

Another method used to create the seed set was described as "judgmental sampling." This involved a review of Boolean keyword searches, with the top 50 hits being coded. The nonprivileged results would be produced so that the plaintiffs could check the defendants' coding for relevance. The defendants also used additional keywords provided by the plaintiffs that resulted in review and tagging of another 4,000 documents. The review was to be performed by "senior attorneys," as opposed to paralegals or more junior lawyers.[21]

The defendants' counsel would do iterative rounds to "stabilize the training of the software." The vendor would rank the relevance of documents with a score of 0 to 100. The defendants suggested seven rounds, in each of which they would review at least 500 documents from different "concept clusters" to see if new documents were being returned. Then they would review a random sample from the documents designated as nonrelevant for testing purposes. In yet another nod to transparency, they would show the plaintiffs all of the documents "looked at," including those deemed nonrelevant.[22]

The plaintiffs' vendor had conflicting feelings and stated, "[W]e don't at this point agree that this is going to work. This is new technology and it has to be proven out." But at the same time the vendor representative stated, "[I]t is fair to say [that] we are big proponents of it." And the court opined that it "works better than most of the alternatives, if not all of the [present] alternatives. So the idea is not to make this perfect, it's not going to be perfect. The idea is to make it significantly better than the alternatives without nearly as much cost."[23] At this point it sounded like everyone involved supported predictive coding and that things might ultimately work themselves out. Alas, this would not prove to be the case. In the plaintiffs' objection to Judge Peck's orders, they claimed that the defendants' protocol was drastically off the mark and "risks failing to capture a staggering 65% of the relevant documents in this case."[24]

While the court ended up accepting the defendants' protocol, it did so with the caveat that it might need to do additional rounds if "weird things" happened. The plaintiffs claimed that the judge had "provide[d] unlawful 'cover' for MSL's counsel" because their duty under FRCP R.26(g)(1)(A) is to certify that production is 'complete' and 'correct.'" Judge Peck did not share their interpretation of the certification rule, stating that the rule requires no such certification of production, and in fact, no lawyer could certify to such completeness and correctness where millions of e-mails are involved. (Rather, according to the court, the certification requirement applies to a "disclosure" in the sense of the mandatory initial disclosure of witnesses and categories of documents that a party will use to support claims and defenses.)[25]

The plaintiffs further objected that no standards of relevance had been established, but the court held that the proposed protocol would provide total transparency into any such determinations and that in any event relevance disputes can be resolved by the court.[26]

The plaintiffs also attacked Judge Peck's opinion and sought his recusal, in part on the basis of his participation in thought leadership on predictive coding, sometimes jointly with the defendants' counsel and vendor. They note that he "has long been a vocal advocate of predictive coding. In the 10 months between the filing of the Amended Complaint and the February 24 written opinion, Judge Peck authored an article and made no fewer than six public appearances espousing the use of predictive coding. A frequent presence on these panels is [counsel for defendants] in this case—another outspoken predictive coding advocate whom Judge Peck 'know[s] very well.'"[27] The plaintiffs were apparently not amused by Judge Peck's comment on the record that the defendants' counsel "must have thought [they] died and went to heaven" after learning that the case had been assigned to him.[28]

It is still unclear whether the plaintiffs in *Moore* can succeed in upsetting the predictive coding protocol applecart. Regardless, the case is interesting not only because of the notion that a court recognized or approved predictive coding for the first time, but also because of the particular arguments about the proposed protocol. There are issues of transparency, defensibility, proportionality, and cooperation underlying (and overlaying) the heated disputes recorded for posterity in the transcripts, briefs, and opinions associated with the case. Whether the protocol in *Moore* will serve as a model for future predictive coding cases remains to be seen, but the identification of issues is instructive.

## 2.2.2 More Cooperation and Transparency

### 2.2.2.1 *KLEEN PRODUCTS, PROGRESSIVE,* **AND** *BRIDGESTONE* *Kleen Products LLC v. Packaging Corp. of America*[29] is a Sherman Act case involving allegations of antitrust violations in the containerboard industry. In this case, the requesting parties (plaintiffs) demanded that responding parties (defendants) use TAR to respond to their requests, based on the argument that more traditional means of producing documents are less accurate. Ultimately, in keeping with a variety of other cases,[30] Magistrate Judge Nan Nolan directed the parties to develop a mutually agreeable keyword search approach rather than argue over whether predictive coding would be superior.

The plaintiffs wanted the defendants to redo their productions using TAR and to complete all future productions utilizing TAR, which is presumably the same or similar to what they called "content-based advanced analytics." Plaintiffs argued that the Boolean keyword process is:

> . . . subject to the inadequacies and flaws inherent when keywords are used to identify responsive documents. They requested that Defendants use content-based advanced analytics ('CBAA') technology to conduct natural language, subject matter searches across corporate departments or corporate functions, using content-based search technology rather than keywords.[31]

The defendants explained their process for identifying documents as "iterative" and involving working with consultants to revise and refine search terms. The efficacy of these Boolean keyword searches was then tested through sampling. During evidentiary hearings, the plaintiffs asserted that this search methodology would likely find less than 25% of responsive documents in contrast with their content-based advance analytics. They claimed that this more advanced technology would find more than 70% of responsive documents without an increase in cost. This was ostensibly true because the technology "do[es] not focus on matching words but instead on identifying relevant concepts out of the documents."[32] In what would prove to be a fatal flaw in their arguments, however, the plaintiffs were not able to identify any missing documents or other holes in the defendants' production.

The defendants contradicted this claim of superior accuracy based on their "testing and validations processes." They stated that the processes ensured "a degree of accuracy that meets or surpasses not only industry standards but also the likely accuracy of any other available methodology."[33] Note that at this point, the defendants had already produced more than a million documents, so any "do over" would have meant significant additional spending. Moreover, the defendants claimed that notwithstanding the plaintiffs' demand for content-based advanced analytics, they had already used TAR in the form of tools such as domain filtering and e-mail threading.[34] In a cooperative vein, they allowed the plaintiffs to participate in choosing keywords and used a sampling testing protocol to measure quality.[35]

Both parties elicited expert testimony during the two days of evidentiary hearings. Nonetheless, after two days, the Court cited Sedona Principle 6 for the proposition that "[r]esponding parties are best situated to evaluate the procedures, methodologies, and techniques appropriate for preserving and producing their own electronically stored information."[36] Many other courts have reached the same conclusion in cases that do not involve predictive coding.[37]

The Judge directed that the parties attempt to reach a compromise on Boolean search: "[T]he defendants had done a lot of work, the defendant under Sedona 6 has the right to pick the [electronic discovery] method. Now, we all know, every court in the country has used Boolean search, I mean, this is not like some freak thing that they [defendants] picked out. . ."[38]

Moreover, Judge Nolan held that the plaintiffs had no basis trying to tell the defendants which technology they should be using without identifying any indications that the production was insufficient. "[W]hat I was learning from the two days, and this is something no other court in the country has really done too, is how important it is to have quality search. I mean, if we want to use the term 'quality' or 'accurate,' but we all want this . . . how do you verify the work that you have done already, is the way I put it."

The court explicitly addressed the notion that "cooperation" is not in conflict with the lawyer's duty to advocate for the client as follows:

> _Lawyers have twin duties of loyalty: While they are retained to be zealous advocates for their clients, they bear a professional obligation to conduct discovery in a diligent and candid manner. Their combined duty is to strive in the best interests of their clients to achieve the best results at a reasonable cost, with integrity and candor as officers of the court. Cooperation does not conflict with the advancement of their clients' interests—it enhances it. Only when lawyers confuse advocacy with adversarial conduct are these twin duties in conflict. The Sedona Conference, The Sedona Conference Cooperation Proclamation, 10 Sedona Conf. J. 331, 331 (2009)._

There ensued five months of meeting and conferring, leading to a stipulated order. In the stipulated order,[39] the plaintiffs withdrew their demand that defendants apply content-based advanced analytics with respect to certain document productions and requests. However, the order provides that with respect to certain documents identified as newly collected documents, "the parties will meet and confer regarding the appropriate search methodology to be used." If no agreement is reached, the parties are permitted to file a motion with the Court. Moreover, there is a broad provision stating that the plaintiffs have not waived:

> _[A]ny additional objections they may have to defendants' search methodology for the First Requests, including any additional objections relating to defendants' identification, collection, custodians, data sources, search terms, statistical validation, review or production of documents, and that defendants' objections to the First Request unduly narrowed the scope of responsive documents, and defendants will not argue or contend that plaintiffs, in whole or in part, have waived or otherwise failed to fully reserve such additional objections by entering into this Stipulation._[40]

Not to be outdone, the "[d]efendants reserve all rights they currently have with respect to their position that their document collection and production efforts met or exceeded relevant legal standards."[41]

The court terminated further evidentiary hearings based on the stipulation, effectively leaving us all in perpetual suspense.

The dangers of proceeding with TAR after agreeing to a discovery protocol that does not contemplate TAR are starkly illustrated in _Progressive Cas. Ins. Co. v. Delaney,_ *et al.,* 2014 WL 2112927 (D.Nev.). In *Progressive,* the parties agreed to an ESI protocol that involved the application of search terms to the plaintiff's ESI and subsequent review and production. The protocol was arrived at amidst much meeting and conferring, as well as discovery motion practice.

However, after beginning manual review of the hits resulting from application of the agreed search terms, the plaintiff decided that it would be more effective and cost-efficient to apply predictive coding to those hits instead. The opinion contains extensive discussion of the history of the parties' interactions on e-discovery, but the bottom line is that the court disapproved of the plaintiff's decision to apply predictive coding after having agreed to an ESI protocol that did not include it. Plaintiff's failure to meet several agreed upon production deadlines appears to have also dampened the court's mood. The court also found fault with the methodology employed, citing, among other things, the best practices published by the vendor of the TAR software plaintiff used as well as the plaintiff's expert.

*Progressive* is noteworthy for the level of transparency the court holds forth as required for the use of TAR. Citing, *inter alia, Da Silva Moore* as supporting authority, the court states that production of "seed sets" is required. It also states that the use of TAR is only permitted where full transparency is given. The court summarizes these transparency and cooperation issues as follows:

> *The cases which have approved technology assisted review of ESI have required an unprecedented degree of transparency and cooperation. . . . In the handful of cases that have approved technology assisted review of ESI, the courts have required the producing party to provide the requesting party with full disclosure about the technology used, the process, and the methodology, including the documents used to "train" the computer. . . . [L]itigators are loathe to reveal their methodological decisions for various reasons including assertions that: methodological decisions reveal work product; discovery about discovery exceeds the scope of Rule 26 of the Federal Rules of Procedure; revealing documents nonresponsive to discovery requests exposes the producing party to unnecessary litigation risks; and the Federal Rules of Civil Procedure only require parties to conduct a reasonable search for responsive documents.*

The use of TAR methodologies not previously contemplated by the parties is also addressed in *Bridgestone Americas, Inc. v. Int'l Bus. Machines Corp.,* No. 3:13-1196, ECF #89 (M.D. Tenn. July 22, 2014). In Bridgestone, the plaintiff sought to use predictive coding to review over two million documents for responsiveness after an initial screening had been completed via the use of search terms.

The court allowed the modification of the discovery schedule to accommodate the use of predictive coding, acknowledging the fact that it was "allowing Plaintiff to switch horses in midstream." However, not like *Progressive,* where the court noted patterns of noncooperation and missed deadlines by plantiff, the court in *Bridgestone* referenced the "critical importance" of "openness and transparency" on the part of Bridgestone. *Id. slip op at 2.* Similarly, the court noted that "[b]oth parties have expressed an interest in keeping this case moving and preserving the trial date..." *Id.*

*slip op at 3*. The Magistrate Judge also held open the option for Defendant to switch to predictive coding.

Two additional cases revisit the "transparency and cooperation" elements outlined in *Progressive*. In *Dynamo Holding L. P. et al. v. Comm'r of Internal Rev., 143 T.C. No. 9, 2014 WL 4636526 (U.S. Tax Ct. Sept. 17, 2014)*, the court held that, "[w]here, as here, petitioners reasonably request to use predictive coding to conserve time and expense, and represent to the Court that they will retain electronic discovery experts to meet with respondent's counsel or his experts to conduct a search acceptable to respondent, we see no reason petitioners should not be allowed to use predictive coding to respond to respondent's discovery request."

Similarly, the court in *Good v. American Water Works, No. 2:14-cv-01374 (S.D.W. Va. Oct. 29, 2014)* focused on transparency and cooperation in its analysis as to whether a Rule 502(d) protective order was sufficient that the producing party should not be allowed to engage in additional privilege review after predictive coding. Defendants viewed the order as "encourage[ing] the incorporation" of predictive coding, while Plaintiffs considered it as "disallowing linear (aka 'eyes on') privilege review altogether." The court entered the Defendant's proposed Rule 502(d) order, citing the expectation that defendants would ensure delays "will uniformly be minimized." *Id. at 6*. The court also allowed that "undue delay" would be cause for the Plaintiffs to seek amendment to the order.

Decisions like *Progressive* and its progeny are upsetting to those who maintain that discovery methods should only be questioned where the requesting party can demonstrate, based on facts, that there is some deficiency with the production. Courts like the *Progressive* court are putting a stake in the ground. To these courts, TAR simply cannot exist without full transparency and full cooperation. However, as shown by the holding in Bridgestone, courts are likely to provide greater latitude regarding the modification of ESI protocols when parties act in accord with transparency and cooperation.

## 2.2.3 Burden and Proportionality

### 2.2.3.1 *BIOMET, FOSAMAX,* AND *INDEPENDENT LIVING CENTER OF SOUTHERN CALIFORNIA* Similarly, in *In Re: Biomet M2a Magnum Hip Implant Products Liability Litigation*,[42] a hip implant products liability case, the plaintiffs argued that *Biomet* should have used TAR from the initial stages of its ESI review. *Biomet* started its efforts to filter its original universe of ESI by applying keyword searching then deduplicated the remainder and only then applied TAR to what was left. The court ruled that this process satisfied *Biomet's* discovery obligations.

The parties had jointly identified a population of 19.5 million to search for relevance.[43] They also agreed on protocols to "facilitate identification, retrieval, and production of ESI." *Biomet* asserted that its production method was consistent with these protocols.

The initial stage of keyword searching reduced the originally identified 19.5 million documents down to 3.9 million, equivalent to 1.5 terabytes, constituting 16%

of the original 19.5 million. Subsequent application of deduplication further lowered the population to 2.5 million. Finally, TAR was applied to cull relevant ESI from the 2.5 million documents that were left.[44]

*Biomet* then performed a statistical analysis to validate its results. Reportedly, sampling showed a 99% confidence rate that between 0.55% and 1.33% of the documents to which TAR was applied were responsive and that (with the same confidence rate indicated) between 1.37% and 2.47% of the original 19.5 million documents were responsive. The costs associated with the production were reported to be $1.07 million at the time the motion papers were submitted, and *Biomet* estimated that when complete the costs would be between $2 million and $3.25 million.[45]

Plaintiffs averred that *Biomet* had produced only a fraction of the relevant documents. They argued that published research and scholarship has established the relative inaccuracy of keyword searching to TAR. Accordingly, they asserted that the keyword search had "tainted" the entire process. They declined *Biomet*'s offer to suggest additional keyword search terms, claiming that it would be impractical because the plaintiffs were unfamiliar with *Biomet*'s terminology. The only way the plaintiffs believed the process could be fixed was to start again from the beginning and apply TAR to the entire original universe of 19.5 million documents.[46]

The court rejected the plaintiffs' demands based on, *inter alia*, proportionality grounds, in light of the results of *Biomet*'s sampling and the projected cost of complying with the plaintiffs' demands:

> *Even in light of the needs of the hundreds of plaintiffs in this case, the very large amount in controversy, the parties' resources, the importance of the issues at stake, and the importance of this discovery in resolving the issues, I can't find that the likely benefits of the discovery proposed by the Steering Committee equals or outweighs its additional burden on, and additional expense to, Biomet. FED. R. CIV. P. 26(b)(2)(C).*[47]

*In re Biomet* is another case where the requesting party, presumably the party with the strongest interest in receiving a complete production, was pushing for expanded, comprehensive, and even retroactive use of TAR. Indeed, the requesting party argued that the failure to use TAR from the beginning "tainted" the entire process. This is a stark demonstration of the fact that TAR is not only appealing to defendants with large volumes of ESI who are concerned with reducing cost, but also to requesting parties who are interested in receiving a complete and accurate production.

The *Fosamax* case is a similar situation.[48] The defendant had produced about 11 million documents, and the plaintiff wanted it to redo the entire production using predictive coding. The court rejected this request because the plaintiff had shown no material deficiency in the production.

The issues of burden and proportionality again present themselves in *Independent Living Center of Southern California*, where the dispute centers on "whether quality assurance should be used to test the reliability" of the predictive coding system. *Id slip op at 2*. As a secondary issue, there was a dispute as to who should bear the cost of that quality assurance.

In this case, defendant had 2,000,000 documents requiring searching and estimates of approximately 250,000 documents resulting from those searches. Plaintiff's advocated for keyword searching or review of the documents. *Id. slip op at 3.* However, the court ordered the use of predictive coding, to be paid for by Defendant, and the parties agreed on the use of Equivio. Plaintiff was entitled to the top 10,000 most responsive documents and could seek additional responsive documents at Plaintiff's expense. However, experts for the parties disagreed on the importance of "quality assurance," as well as its time required to perform that task. *Id. slip op at 2.*

The court concluded that plaintiffs could insist on quality assurance, but were required to pay half the cost for it. The court considered this a "middle ground" short of denying the disputed step entirely. *Id. slip op at 2.*

## 2.2.3.2 JUDICIAL ENCOURAGEMENT OF TAR AS A WAY TO REDUCE BURDEN— *CHEVRON* AND *HARRIS SUBCONTRACTING*

**2.2.3.2.1 *Chevron*** Parties making burden objections to electronic discovery requests may find judges suggesting that predictive coding can alleviate their burdens.[49] One example is *Chevron Corp. v. Donziger*,[50] involving a subpoena to a nonparty, albeit one with close connections to the litigation. The *Chevron* court did what several other courts are doing (anecdotally at least), that is, to "encourage" the parties to use predictive coding. The court indicated that counsel had "overstated the burden of compliance, in terms both of the cost and the required time and has avoided engaging with options that give strong promise of reducing that cost and burden."[51]

As evidence of this, the court pointed to its urging at a hearing for "the parties to analyze, in their subsequent submissions with respect to burden, whether and to what extent predictive coding could 'reduce the burden and effort' required to comply with the Subpoena." The court then took counsel to task for ignoring the subject notwithstanding the court's suggestion (which is never a good idea). According to the court, "The logical inference is that [counsel] failed to address the subject because it would not have aided its argument."[52]

The lawyers' burden estimates were premised on the assumption that each document would be reviewed at least twice by the firm's attorneys. This review was estimated to take 15 to 20 lawyers working 40-hour weeks over 40 weeks. Moreover, counsel estimated that 15% of the documents would be reviewed a third time by senior attorneys. The court had its own ideas about how to conduct the review, seeing "no legitimate reason why (1) far less costly contract attorneys could not do all or most of the review, as is common in the legal community today, (2) two or certainly three levels of review are necessary, or (3) more reviewers could not be used."[53]

Counsel estimated review cost between $1,060,000 and $1,290,000. However, the court found that even assuming the accuracy of this estimate, the cost would not constitute an undue burden considering such proportionality factors as "[the non-party's role in this case, its size (reportedly over $300 million in gross revenues in 2012), and its economic interest in this controversy . . . Indeed, there is no persuasive evidence that the compliance costs are out of line with what would be typical for nonparty witness in complex commercial litigation."[54] With the availability and judicial recommendation of predictive coding in the backdrop, the court also declined to shift any costs to the requesting party.

**2.2.3.2.2 Harris**    In *Harris v. Subcontracting Concepts, LLC*, another federal court in New York considering a subpoena rejected a burden objection in part due to the availability of predictive coding.[55] The court recognized that the amount of information requested was "enormous" and reduced the scope of the subpoena and "imposed representative sampling." With respect to discovery of the ESI at issue, the Court stated that "the amount of time, cost, and effort expended to produce these records from the computer is significantly less than by hand. With the advent of software, predictive coding, spreadsheets, and similar advances, the time and cost to produce large reams of documents can be dramatically reduced."[56] Taking these technological advantages, the court was convinced that there was no undue burden.

## 2.2.4 *Hinterberger*—Arguing about Cooperation

In many electronic discovery cases, and especially in predictive coding disputes, courts have been outspoken about the need to cooperate.[57] The problem with mandates to cooperate is that lawyers are uncooperative about how to apply it. *Hinterberger, et al. v. Catholic Health Systems, Inc.*[58] is just such a case where lawyers fight about cooperation.[59] In fact, the plaintiff moved for an order that the defendants cooperate, specifically that they "engage in meaningful meet and confer discussions regarding an ESI protocol with both parties' respective ESI experts/consultants; and an order that if the parties are unable to agree upon an ESI protocol by a deadline set by the court, that each side submit its own proposed ESI protocol to the court for a ruling as to which protocol should be adopted in this case."[60]

In its decision, the court recounts a difficult year during the course of which the parties tried to agree on how the defendants should review their e-mails on the basis of keyword search. Like other courts in other cases discussed here, the *Hinterberger* court suggested that the parties use predictive coding. The court asked the parties to submit proposed protocols for keyword search methodology. The defendants then decided to abandon a keyword approach and use predictive coding, seeking to confer with the plaintiff as to identification of relevant custodians.[61]

The defendants had provided the plaintiffs with a proposed protocol for predictive coding. The plaintiffs objected to the proposed protocol, raising issues that they wanted to discuss with technical consultants and cooperatively resolve before defendants went ahead with implementing their protocol. Plaintiffs went so far as to argue that the law requires a party intending to use predictive coding to negotiate a protocol and that defendants had refused to discuss the protocol with them. They also argued that the defendants had not complied with the necessary transparency in the level of detail they had disclosed about their predictive coding plans, including their seed set, citing the *Moore* opinion discussed above.[62]

The defendants argued that the plaintiffs' objections were premature and rejected their characterization of *Moore* as requiring the production of the seed set. The plaintiffs apparently backed off the latter contention but didn't waiver on cooperation. In addition to citing cases where courts ordered parties to meet and confer with respect to electronic discovery searches, they pointed to a local rule requiring that parties "discuss and attempt to reach agreement as to the method of searching" for ESI. The plaintiffs asked the court to issue a reminder in the nature of a warning to the defendants that even if the instant motion was not granted, their methodology could be found unreasonable and noncompliant with their Rule 34 obligations.[63]

The defendants decided that they would meet and confer with plaintiffs regarding their use of predictive coding, which was probably the safer posture to take, and the court decided that a warning was unnecessary. Given the evaporation of the putative failure to cooperate, the court decided to decline to further address the plaintiffs' objections to the defendants' predictive coding protocol.[64] It appears that cooperation is a hard thing to argue against when it comes to predictive coding.

### 2.2.5 *EORHB*—*sua sponte* TAR (or not)

While it is an interesting but not completely shocking development that courts are encouraging the use of predictive coding as a way to deal with the problem of voluminous electronic discovery, it could be another matter entirely if the courts started ordering parties to use predictive coding over their objections. In *EORHB, Inc.*[65] the court issued an order that made big waves because it seemed to be the first *sua sponte* order requiring that the parties use predictive coding.

The court's October 15, 2012, order provided that "[a]bsent a modification of this order for good cause shown, the parties shall (i) retain a single discovery vendor to be used by both sides, and (ii) conduct document review with the assistance of predictive coding."[66] This exciting and controversial development was short lived, however, as a few months later the court issued another order noting, *inter alia*, that the parties had agreed that there was no need for them to use the same discovery platform and that "based on the low volume of relevant documents expected to be produced in discovery by [plaintiffs], the cost of using predictive coding assistance would likely be outweighed by any practical benefit of its use." Accordingly, the order provided that the "[p]laintiffs and [d]efendants shall not be required to retain a single discovery vendor to be used by both sides" and that the "[p]laintiffs may conduct document review using traditional methods."[67] Accordingly, it does not appear that a court has required *unwilling parties* to use predictive coding, and it may be a long time before one does.

## 2.3 Conclusion

So far courts do not seem to have taken the step of ordering that parties use predictive coding. However, they are encouraging it in a way that may make it hard for parties to resist. Requesting parties are also recognizing that they may benefit by the improved accuracy enabled by TAR and demanding that it be used to identify responsive documents for production. Where parties are proposing the use of predictive coding, courts are expecting at least some degree of transparency, proportionality, and behavior that does not come naturally for litigators in an adversarial system—cooperation.

# Notes

1. Doug Laney, "3-D Data Management: Controlling Data Volume, Velocity, and Variety," February 6, 2001 (blogs.gartner.com/doug-laney/files/2012/01/ad949-3DDataManagement-Controlling-Data-Volume-Velocity-and-Variety.pdf).
2. *Da Silva Moore v. Publicis Groupe*, 2012 U.S. Dist. LEXIS 23350 (SDNY, Feb. 24, 2012).
3. *Kleen Products v. Packaging Corp. of America*, 2012 U.S. Dist. LEXIS 139632 (ND Ill. Sep. 28, 2012). Judge Peck distinguished the cases on the basis that in his case, the parties had agreed to use predictive coding, while in *Kleen Products* the issue of whether to use predictive coding was the subject of dispute. The plaintiffs in *Moore* took issue with his characterization of their agreement.
4. See Adam I. Cohen and David J. Lender, *Electronic Discovery: Law and Practice* (2d. Ed. 2013), §2.04.
5. *Id.*, at §2.09[A][2]-[3].
6. 10 Sedona Conf. J. 331 (2009 Supp.).
7. *Da Silva Moore v. Publicis Groupe*, 2012 U.S. Dist. LEXIS 23350 (SDNY, Feb. 24, 2012).
8. See *id.* at 3. An April 23, 2012 order in *Global Aerospace Inc., et al. v. Landow Aviation, L.P. d/b/a Dulles Jet Center, et al.*, Consolidated Case No. CL 61040 (Virginia, Loudoun County Circuit Court), permitted the use of predictive coding over the objection of the requesting party but preserved the requesting party's rights to question the completeness of the production. See also, *The New Mexico State Investment Council v. Bland, et. al.*, 2014 WL 772860 (N.M. Dist.) (approving factual investigation underpinning settlements conducted in part using TAR).
9. *Da Silva Moore v. Publicis Groupe*, 2012 U.S. Dist. LEXIS 23350, at 3 (SDNY, Feb. 24, 2012).
10. See *id.* at 4.
11. See *id.*
12. See *id.* at 4-5.
13. See *id.* at 5.
14. Plaintiffs' reply objecting to Judge Peck's Feb. 8, 2012 Discovery Rulings at 3, *Da Silva Moore v. Publicis Groupe*, No. 11 Civ. 1279(ALC)(AJP), 2012 WL 517207 (S.D.N.Y. Feb. 14, 2012), ECF No. 51.
15. *Kleen Products v. Packaging Corp. of America*, 2012 U.S. Dist. LEXIS 139632 (ND Ill. Sep. 28, 2012).

16. *Da Silva Moore v. Publicis Groupe*, 2012 U.S. Dist. LEXIS 23350, at 10 (SDNY, Feb. 24, 2012).

17. *Victor Stanley, Inc. v. Creative Pipe, Inc.*, 250 F.R.D. 251, 260 n.10 (D. Md. 2008).

18. *Da Silva Moore v. Publicis Groupe*, 2012 U.S. Dist. LEXIS 23350, at 6 (SDNY, Feb. 24, 2012) (citing various portions of 1/4/12 Conf. Tr.).

19. See *id.* at 5-6.

20. See *id.* at 7.

21. See *id.* at 7.

22. See *id.*

23. See *id.*

24. See *id.* at 6.

25. *Da Silva Moore II*, No. 11 Civ. 1279(ALC)(AJP), 2012 WL 607412, at 3 (S.D.N.Y. Feb. 24, 2012).

26. *Da Silva Moore v. Publicis Groupe*, 2012 U.S. Dist. LEXIS 23350, at 10-11 (SDNY, Feb. 24, 2012).

27. Plaintiffs' Notice of Motion for Recusal or Disqualification, *Da Silva Moore III*, 2012 WL 1446534 (No. 11 Civ. 1279(ALC)(AJP)), ECF No. 169).

28. Transcript of Dec. 2, 2011 Conference at 8, *Da Silva Moore v. Publicis Groupe*, No. 11 Civ. 1279(ALC)(AJP), 2012 WL 517207 (S.D.N.Y. Feb. 14, 2012), ECF No. 51.

29. *Kleen Products v. Packaging Corp. of America*, 2012 U.S. Dist. LEXIS 139632 (ND Ill. Sep. 28, 2012).

30. See footnote 4, *supra*.

31. *Kleen Products v. Packaging Corp. of America*, 2012 U.S. Dist. LEXIS 139632 at 5 (ND Ill. Sep. 28, 2012).

32. See *id.* at 6.

33. *See id.* at 5.

34. See *id.* at 5-6.

35. See *id.* at 6.

36. *The Sedona Conference Best Practices Commentary on the Use of Search and Information Retrieval Methods in E-Discovery*, 8 Sedona Conf. J. 189, 193 (Fall 2007).

37. See footnote 4, *supra*.

38. Transcript of Apr. 2, 2012 Proceedings Before the Honorable Nan Nolan at 12, *Kleen Products*, 2012 WL 4498465 (No. 10 C 5711), ECF No. 319-1.

39. Judge Nolan's August 21, 2012 Stipulation and Order Related to ESI Search, *Kleen Products*, 2012 WL 4498465 (No. 10 C 5711), ECF No. 319-1 (attached in the Appendix to this chapter). Also attached is the protocol from *In Re: Actos (Pioglitazone) Products Liability Litigation*, 2012 US Dist. LEXIS 187519 (WD La. Jul. 27, 2012).

40. See *id.* at 18.

41. See *id.*

42. *In Re: Biomet M2A Magnum Hip Implant Products Liability Litigation*, 2013 WL 1729682 (N.D. Ind. Apr. 18, 2013).

43. See *id.* at 1.

44. See *id.*

45. See *id.* at 2.

46. See *id.*

47. See *id.* at 3.

48. *Fosamax Alendronate Sodium Drug Cases*, No. JCCP 4644 (Orange Co. Cal. Sup. Ct.) (April 18, 2013).

49. These judges include the Hon. Shira Scheindlin, the judge who has been most closely associated with electronic discovery. *See National Day Laborer Organizing Network et al. v. United States Immigration and Customs Enforcement Agency, et al.* 2012 U.S. Dist. Lexis 97863 (SDNY, July 13, 2012) (*"Through iterative learning, these methods (known as 'computer-assisted' or 'predictive' coding) allow humans to teach computers what documents are and are not responsive to a particular FOIA or discovery request and they can significantly increase the effectiveness and efficiency of searches."*)

50. *Chevron Corp. v. Donziger*, 11 Civ. 0691, 2013 U.S. Dist. LEXIS 36353 (S.D.N.Y. Mar. 15, 2013).

51. See *id.* at 36.

52. See *id.*

53. See *id.*

54. See *id.* at 37.

55. *Harris v. Subcontracting Concepts*, LLC, 2013 U.S. Dist. LEXIS 33593 (NDNY, Mar. 11, 2013).

56. See *id.* at 4.

57. See, e.g., *Ruiz-Bueno, III v. Scott*, No. 2:12-cv-0809, 2013 WL 6055402 (S.D. Ohio Nov. 15, 2013). In this case, the court deemed "discovery about discovery" permissible, ordering Defendants to produce information as to what methods were used to search for responsive electronically stored information.

58. *Hinterberger, et al. v. Catholic Health System, Inc., et al.*, 08-CV-380S(F), 2013 U.S. Dist. LEXIS 73141 (W.D.N.Y. May 21, 2013).

59. Ironically, the wisdom of establishing an explicit rule that lawyers cooperate has been the subject of debate, with many lawyers arguing that expressly mandating cooperation will lead to satellite litigation over whether the appropriate level of cooperation has been satisfied.

60. See *id.* at 2.

61. See *id.* at 3.

62. See *id.* at 5.

63. See *id.* at 6.

64. See *id.* at 7.

65. *EORHB, Inc., et al. v. HOA Holdings, LLC*, 2013 WL 1960621 (Del. Ch.).

66. See *id.* at 1.

67. See *id.*

# CHAPTER 3

# The Economics of TAR

## 3.1 Overview

Document review consumes roughly 73% of the average budget for document production.[1] Due to the continued widespread use of linear review, that average remains stubbornly higher than it need be. Any meaningful analysis of the relative costs of document review must take into account all costs and savings for services and software. These include the frequently overlooked costs to manage and support the review process—particularly important for large-scale linear reviews—in addition to the typically budgeted costs of platform licenses and document reviewers.

The value of TAR is often expressed in terms of cost reduction, and indeed it has proven highly effective as a means of lowering the costs of document review compared to linear review. At the same time, many of the cases discussed in Chapter 2 cite overall effectiveness as a more compelling driver for TAR implementation, particularly for requesting parties. Unfortunately, there is no universal definition of effectiveness in this context; some parties measure effectiveness based on the ability to find valuable documents at the lowest cost; others are more interested in the overall cost of completing one's obligation adequately. Proportionality arguments and cost-shifting can further flummox efforts to weigh cost savings and effectiveness.

## 3.2 Defining Cost Metrics

Meaningful cost analysis requires creation of a granular model to detail expected areas of costs. A number of vendors have made estimators available online, as has the EDRM,[2] in order to provide greater transparency into pricing and its application to specific finite scenarios.

The challenge for stakeholders is that these models are only as good their ability to reflect reality, and reality as it unfolds in electronic discovery often diverges from assumptions in the model, since it is driven by facts and circumstances, and dynamic events, unique to each case. It is important to establish a framework that includes a range of possible values and a rationale for that range, typically based on past experience with similar data sets and matter types as well as on measurable attributes of the existing data to determine what meaningful metrics are available for creating a realistic budget.

## 3.2.1 Interrelationship of Electronic Discovery and TAR Economics

TAR technology does not exist in a vacuum. How it is deployed and how it is priced depend on the ecosystem in which TAR is implemented. The upstream processes that typically precede TAR in electronic discovery are preservation, collection, early data assessment, processing, and hosting, but TAR can also be used in most of these earlier steps. Even as the EDRM is evolving to reflect the convergence of many of these steps, the multiple ways TAR can be deployed in the process make clearheaded modeling of alternatives a must for any meaningful economic decision support. For example, is TAR to be used as part of an integrated managed document review service that bundles attorney review time with a hosting platform that includes review; or as part of a primary platform solution used throughout a matter; or as an early data assessment (EDA) solution upstream from hosting; or in some other capacity?

In turn, the accountability for how TAR performs may include numerous participants in that ecosystem. In systems that rely on seed sets, the effectiveness of mining the data, seed-set searching, and the initial review of document samples are multiplied many times over. In systems that rely on a truly random sample to start the process, the amount of responsive material found and the consistency of the initial review play a very disproportionate role in the overall cost, impacting the number and size of future sampling rounds and the amount of material that is confidently classified (thus averting "eyes on" review) versus the amount that is classified with low confidence through techniques such as ad hoc searching.

Electronic discovery product vendors and service providers tend to focus on implementation of off-the-shelf TAR technologies, often with fixed acquisition costs. The purchaser must mindfully include the human capital and infrastructure costs necessary to configure, deploy and operate the products to perform as required. This option is most commonly seen in very large organizations with repetitive and somewhat predictable legal dockets, where maintaining a higher overhead for electronic discovery efforts is a suitable (if not required) cost of doing business. In addition, a prudent evaluation will also take into account the potential costs associated with systemic error and delays introduced during the implementation process.

Electronic discovery service providers also tend to offer fee-for-service models that allow pay-as-you-go purchasing of individual services anchored by certain products or product classes and allocation of their fixed costs over multiple client projects. Fees are often a combination of "a la carte" prices driven by volume and count (e.g., per GB, per document, per hour). An increasingly common trend is for companies to negotiate a bundled pricing solution that provides predictable costs up to a certain set of limits in return for discounts, incentives, or service-level agreements. Overall, the primary cost-driver in this model is typically data volume; yet even in those types of arrangements, a growing number of buyers are seeking alternative metrics such as custodian count, claim count, or deadline compliance as the basis of payment.

In another increasingly common trend, electronic discovery companies and some law firms are incorporating TAR into a service offering specifically designed to handle document review—a service offering often called "Managed Document Review" (MDR). MDR providers can either augment electronic discovery offerings (such as data processing and data hosting) or subsume them.

In augmenting an offering, the MDR providers might charge a "per document" fee for managed review, over and above the cost of an electronic discovery platform and services delivered by a separate vendor. On the other hand, because of the monumental impact that TAR has on the efficiency of every variety of review, especially MDR, many MDR providers are unwilling to hand off the TAR component of their business to a third-party provider and instead opt to incorporate MDR services into a broader pricing model, with a broader range of EDRM steps. Overall, the primary cost driver in this model is usually document count rather than volume in GBs, but many buyers and sellers continue to use hourly pricing for review services in concert with the count or volume-based pricing for TAR.

## 3.2.2 Pricing Models and Budgets

Volumes and document counts drive cost in most instances, even when hourly charges are the predominant unit of billing for providers. Building a realistic budget usually means asking each provider to list every line item that could conceivably be on an invoice and estimating the lowest and highest reasonable estimates for the count in each line item. In addition, it means capturing dependencies. If "per document" pricing is in use, it is critical to define precisely when and how the document count will be established. Is it the collected count? Deduplicated count? Count after removing operating system files? Reviewable subset? Or some other metric?

If "per GB" pricing is used, it is critical to define precisely when and how the volume will be measured. If a bundled pricing arrangement is used and contains provisions for certain volume discounts or triggers, it is critical to define how those volumes will be measured and precisely what additional fees or discounts will be incurred when they are exceeded. Finally, the manner of calculation of any such additional fees or discounts should also be defined.

## 3.2.3 Cost Per Document

Regardless of the pricing model, it is often useful to evaluate evidentiary value on a "per document" basis. When all documents in a matter have been reviewed, they generally fall into stratification similar to the one below. Though the precise categories in a given matter may vary, the concept is to establish rank by value, with a steep pyramid reflecting:

- A handful of deposition and trial exhibits at the very top (that often bring novel clarity to the issue or succinctly distill complex information into a "story" element)
- A few hundred to a few thousand "hot documents" (deemed by counsel as highly responsive whether helpful or harmful to the client's position)
- A larger production set consisting of the putative responsive, nonprivileged documents (deemed sufficiently responsive to specific document requests or relevant to certain issues to merit production)
- An even larger set of "potentially responsive" documents filtered and staged for review
- A very large set of documents that were collected and processed but filtered out prior to defining the reviewable set or included in the reviewable set but coded nonresponsive

The question is: Cost per document for which group?

The most basic analysis suggests that the economic value of review is in determining which of these categories applies to each document. This approach values the decision making process over the outcome of the decision (is this document responsive?) and is often reduced to a "cost per document" based on the total population of the reviewable set, regardless of the disposition of each individual item. This approach makes for a particularly easy assessment of the impact of the TAR compared to linear review if the provider is charging "per document" in the reviewable set.

An alternative approach is to assign costs by tier, calculating a "cost per exhibit," "cost per hot document," "cost per produced document," and so on. The most basic tiered cost implementation in electronic discovery is a two-tier model that uses "GBs in" and "GBs out" based on culling prior to review. In this model, there is a fee (alternately referred to as culling, EDA, preprocessing, indexing, and other similar terms) that applies to all collected data, and a subsequent additional fee that applies only to data that will be "promoted" to the review platform to become part of the reviewable set. This prevalent model is often used in concert with TAR, but holds some tension in that the essential value of TAR—as has been described in various parts of this book—is to leverage seen and unseen attributes of documents to ascertain their appropriate classification. In contrast, this bifurcated approach removes large volumes of documents from consideration based on keywords or other means prior to the application of TAR.

However, this commonly used model does set a precedent for establishing different values for documents at different points in the discovery process. It is only a small logical step to place a higher value on responsive documents than is placed on nonresponsive ones, an even higher value on "hot" documents, and so on. Another useful metric to gauge the efficiency of production is the total cost expended per exhibit, calculated by adding up all fees paid to electronic discovery service providers and document review service providers (including law firms or outside counsel fees for lawyers overseeing the effort), and dividing that sum by the number of exhibits (e.g., deposition, motion, trial, etc.). In a hypothetical matter with a $500,000 spend and 200 deposition exhibits, the cost per deposition exhibit would be $2,500.

It could be argued that this is not really the most useful metric, because parties are obligated to produce the responsive and nonprivileged documents regardless of what exhibits are used. Under this theory, the produced set would be the best set to measure. In our hypothetical example with a $500,000 spend and a produced set of 50,000 documents, the cost per produced document would be $10.

The relative utility of certain metrics may vary in any given case, by client, situation, or otherwise. The key issue is to define the measures that will be meaningful to the matter at hand and track them consistently, to isolate trends over time and to evaluate the ultimate effectiveness of TAR on the total project cost.

### 3.2.4 Pricing, Business Models and Cost Drivers

By contrast, service providers have seen steady erosion in pricing since the advent of electronic discovery, and their ability to maintain profit margins has relied on increasing automation and innovation. Since the late 1990s, electronic discovery service providers have promoted unit-based pricing models as a means to earn profits on the arbitrage of hours to GBs (or pages, or documents, etc.). The compelling rationale for buyers to accept and even demand unit-based pricing (vs. hourly rates) is that they bring a level of certainty based on measurable criteria. But like all business model/pricing issues, the devil is in the details for both buyers and sellers in this market. Common units in the early days of electronic discovery related the work back to familiar paper-based paradigms. Prices reflected the number of "pages" (technically TIF images) that resulted from an electronic collection. In today's digital age it is often very difficult to predict the underlying units (documents/pages per GB or custodian) without first processing the data. This uncertainty necessitates the use of assumptions for unit pricing proposals and often those assumptions are the details that require greater scrutiny.

Today, TAR providers frequently sell software licenses or provide use of their software (often bundled with limited other services) for an incremental "per GB" fee. Providers of integrated TAR in electronic discovery software platforms are often including it as part of the basic fee structure. As noted previously, a key challenge for buyers is to define precisely the data set to which the fee will be applied.

## 3.3 Comparison to Linear Review

For simplicity, throughout this book we have focused on review methods as essentially "single pass" and even noted the judicial objection to a proposed 3-pass (and arguably 4-pass) review proposed in *Chevron Corp. v. Donziger*.[3] However, in traditional linear reviews the process has been broken into steps, frequently utilizing contract attorneys for "first pass" review focused on responsiveness and potential privilege, associates of varying seniority for "second level" review focused on evaluating actual privilege within the presumptively responsive subset of documents, and supervising partners along with contractors, project managers, litigation support specialists, paralegals or other professionals to facilitate the process and design and implement quality assurance measures.

## 3.3.1 First Pass

First pass review comparisons are the easiest to make. Depending on the size and complexity of the matter, first pass review tends to be focused on responsiveness and potential privilege judgments made by staff attorneys, contract attorneys, or associates. The formula to determine cost per document is simply:

$$\text{Hourly rate}/\text{Documents per hour} = \text{Cost per document}$$

For example, a contract attorney at an hourly rate of $50/hour reviewing 50 documents per hour yields a charge of $1/document for first pass review; whereas an associate at a rate of $300/hour reviewing 60 documents per hour yields a charge of $5/document.

It is notable that the sampling work necessary for TAR to be performed effectively often slows down the review rate and requires attorneys who are very familiar with the issues in the case, so a comparison needs to examine not only the averted review ($1/document or $5/document in the examples above), but also the sampling review performed.

If the sampling review requires 7,000 documents over the course of several rounds, and is performed by somewhat more senior associates working at a more deliberate pace, a reasonable cost can be calculated as shown below:

Senior associate at $500/hour reviewing 25 documents per hour yields a charge of $20 per document.

$$7,000 \times \$20 = \$140,000 \text{ for Sampling review}$$

In the same matter, if the TAR process averted review of 500,000 documents at a projected cost of $1/document, the gross savings is $360,000. Of course, to calculate net savings ($360,000) the cost of TAR must include sampling cost ($140,000) before being deducted from the gross savings ($500,000).

The cost benefits achieved through use of TAR diverge from the cost-pattern of linear review as the number of documents increases. Using the assumptions above, if we were to double the number of documents (from 500,000 to 1,000,000), the number of documents required for manual review would also double in number (from 500,000 to 1,000,000); yet the number of samples required to generate a classification model that yields the same standards of measurement should not double— or perhaps even be likely to increase. Sample size does not depend on volume—it depends on variance.

Figure 3.1 is designed to illustrate the kind of divergence that can be achieved as an increasing number of documents are added to the document population. In linear review, the number of documents that need to be reviewed increases linearly at the same incremental pace with the number of documents that need to be coded. With

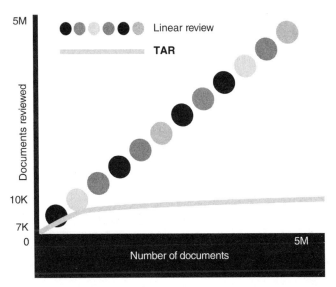

**FIGURE 3.1** Review Burden Comparison between Linear Review and TAR (illustrative)

TAR, the per-document review investment declines significantly as the number of documents increases.

As the number of documents required for human review declines, so does the cost per document. When tens of thousands to millions of documents require review, an appropriate use of TAR can achieve significant savings.

In addition to these direct costs, some indirect costs such as hardware and software or cloud-based infrastructure costs necessarily become part of the overall cost calculus.

## 3.3.2 Second Level/Privilege Review

Privilege poses an especially vexing economic challenge as it is of paramount importance to clients and often requires the attention of the most senior attorneys, because privilege decisions involve more complex legal judgments than responsiveness decisions. Accordingly, privilege decision making tends to be slower, and thus more expensive, than decisions about responsiveness. This was the driving force behind the recent amendments to Federal Rules of Evidence (FRE) Section 502, designed to streamline the privilege review process and create a safe harbor for producing parties who accidentally produce privileged documents, but adhere to the rule's protective criteria.

Privilege review rates tend to rival sampling review rates, and at even greater cost per document because the most senior attorneys tend to be assigned to make final privilege calls. Often, second level review is predicated by both first pass

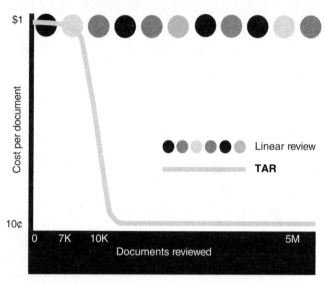

**FIGURE 3.2**   Potential Cost Efficiencies Gained through TAR (illustrative)

review (responsiveness, or in some instances relevance) and a screen for potential privilege.

The screen for potential privilege has historically been a simple key term list comprised of words like "privileged" and "attorney" and so on. Advancements in recent years have included analyzing actors involved in e-mails and other documents to isolate attorneys, clergy, spouses, and others more likely to create a privilege claim in documents. In addition, advanced technologies have evolved to isolate key term hits in documents to differentiate between those that occur in boilerplate language (inherently of lower value) from those that appear in body text. As noted previously, attributes such as typeface and spacing can be taken into account, along with combinations of the above factors to rank the likelihood of a given document being privileged as part of the TAR solution.

From a budgetary perspective, modeling privilege scenarios can be more difficult than modeling for responsiveness. When using TAR, it is straightforward to intersect the predicted responsive results with a privilege screen (privilege language such as "Work Product" and privilege actors such as attorneys and legal e-mail domains); this means there is a dependency in privilege review on the predictive system's ability to precisely categorize responsive documents. For example, if the precision rate for responsiveness is 70%, generally speaking the associated privilege review efficiency will also be 70%.[4] If the precision rate can be raised to 90%, the cost of the privilege review may go down incrementally by about 20%. Once a privilege screen is intersected with the documents predicted to be responsive, the review of the resultant document set can represent a very large portion of total review cost and therefore must be taken into account.

# 3.4 Comparison: TAR to TAR

As noted in the previous chapter, at the time of publication, courts may not be ordering parties to use TAR, but more and more parties are demanding its use, agreeing to its use or choosing to use it unilaterally. Increasingly, their choice is not between linear review and TAR, but between competing TAR solutions.

Many of the TAR to TAR distinctions revolve around the performance of approaches for given data sets; it can be very difficult to evaluate the relative performance of competing solutions. There has been very little objective research into the competing performance on precision and recall, but a recent study conducted by the Electronic Discovery Institute in conjunction with Oracle Corporation[5] sheds light on the subject. Nineteen separate provider solutions were given an identical data set from a closed Oracle matter along with directions related to the objectives of the review; each was given an agreed amount of time with a subject matter expert. The 19 solutions varied wildly in cost and effectiveness. This exercise cost millions of dollars and consumed months of effort for a wide number of stakeholders; it is obviously impractical to replicate it for a given matter.

With that in mind, how can a purchaser of TAR distinguish the costs and benefits of competing approaches and justify a decision based on those results? Realistically, doing so will require relying on representations of providers related to how their technology works and how that approach will best fit a given situation. One way to assess distinct TAR systems is by how successful they are in addressing these and other challenges, especially as comparison of TAR providers replaces comparison of TAR to linear review. But distinct TAR systems are unlikely to address these challenges equally—or in ways that can be communicated clearly and plainly to a nontechnical audience. Discerning buyers will likely require a growing base of knowledge, and/or a trusted and proven adviser to help navigate the best path for a given situation.

# 3.5 Pilot Projects

One increasingly common approach to justifying the economics of TAR is the use of a paid or unpaid pilot project. The most tempting sort of pilot is a "look back" on a closed matter. In a typical corporation, this approach often leads to unwanted consequences. The most problematic is that during the TAR process responsive documents come to light that were not produced previously, creating an ethical conundrum. The second is that rarely does anyone involved put the same level of effort into examining a closed case where the outcome is already known as they do examining an active matter, and as a result the provider often gives far more scrutiny to the matter than the buyer at that point. The third is the "curse of knowledge," meaning that the outcome is in fact known and creates a bias in the process that invalidates the comparison.

An alternative to the "look back" pilot is to use TAR on an active matter with the understanding that all costs will be tracked separately and invoiced after their value is proven. If the premise is that first level review can be eliminated (or dramatically improved) and that adequate quality of first level review uses "agreement" with second level review as a proxy, then it is fairly straightforward to budget for first level review, measure results of TAR on an initial set, and make a valid comparison. If the provider is willing to undertake the initial TAR work on speculation, then the only incremental cost to the buyer for this approach is the rigorous involvement of the expert reviewers doing iterative review of sample sets. This rigorous review arguably should be an ongoing process anyway, reducing the incremental cost to a negligible amount.

This approach has proven highly effective in numerous matters for first-time TAR users seeking to gain hands-on experience with a live matter. The budget is handled by projecting the linear review costs based on agreed assumptions, then paying for TAR at an agreed milestone if it is delivering the promised savings. If not, the linear review would continue at the budgeted amount.

## 3.6 Alternative Value Considerations

Where TAR is deployed determines the magnitude of savings: From enterprise-wide structured initiatives to simple single-case quality control, the value of TAR can be very impactful for a wide variety of circumstances.

For example, as an enabler of better information governance, TAR has the potential to transform enterprise information management by supporting defensible disposition, thus reducing downstream litigation expenses from preservation forward. Over the past decade, many corporations have slashed their discovery costs through rigorous enforcement of records management protocols, keeping only the files necessary for legal, business, tax, and other requirements, and disposing of the rest. Usually these transformations occur on a "going forward" basis, or when major enterprise systems such as e-mail or document management systems are being retired or migrated. However, the potential for TAR to impact this process is much greater when the transformation initiative to "catch up" on records management protocols occurs retrospectively. Many corporations are sitting on hundreds of terabytes of data; using the shorthand convention that one terabyte can be 7.5 million documents, with proper implementation of a review and TAR disposition protocol corporations can save both in terms of upstream maintenance costs and downstream discovery expenses.

### 3.6.1 Multiple Languages

Multilanguage data sets represent special challenges for producing parties. Once data privacy considerations and collection aspects have been addressed, the challenge of reviewing the data becomes multidimensional with the same responsiveness and privilege criteria now being deployed in multiple languages. While the underlying science addresses these challenges from a technical perspective, workflow must be developed to support it and budgets must reflect the additional nuances of that workflow.

A proven approach is to measure the distribution of languages in the data set early in the process to determine whether different languages should be treated differently. If there are vastly different proportions of languages, it is useful to consider where one is most likely to find responsive material, and also how to dispose of a majority of the data. For example, if 5,000 documents are in French and 95,000 are in English, it may make sense to use TAR on the English language documents, then find intersections to the French ones before proceeding with a linear or hybrid review of the French.

In this example, because both are common languages in the United States, it would be relatively trivial to find a sufficient number of bilingual reviewers. However, in large global litigation matters and investigations it is not uncommon to see substantial, interrelated data sets in many languages.

When dealing with these in linear review, it is common to separate languages for different workflows and budgets—for example, Japanese-fluent U.S. attorneys often command higher rates for document review than do French-fluent U.S. attorneys because there is a smaller supply relative to demand. TAR can equalize these imbalances; if a linear review for a given data set would have required 50 French speakers and 50 Japanese speakers, the cost of the Japanese review would have been substantially greater. With TAR, 3 to 5 of each would likely be able to accomplish the task if the proportion of documents in each language remained equal.

## 3.7 Hidden Costs and False Savings

One oft-cited hidden cost of TAR is the admission that a margin of error exists. This concern troubles attorneys who are accustomed to the "gold standard" of 100% linear review, that is, a reasonable process was used to produce results that are inherently acceptable. But as we have seen through a growing number of studies[6] this "gold standard" is increasingly viewed as tarnished. Further, the false sense of security derived from embracing it is misleading because it too can be challenged if there is evidence that it failed to accomplish the objectives. Moreover, it is simply not viable in an ever-larger number of cases because it takes too long and costs too much.

Admitting there is a margin of error may be frightening, but failing to do so is not constructive. The hundreds of matters on which TAR has been used thus far have overcome this hurdle by reducing the margin of error that is present in all document review solutions.

A more substantive concern is that TAR may not reduce costs as much as contemplated because it is applied to the entire universe of potentially responsive documents rather than to a culled subset. The reality is that keyword culling is under increasing scrutiny in light of the power of TAR to find responsive documents in very large data sets. More and more we find that receiving parties will object to the application of keyword filters because of the potentially profound dilution to recall rates across the entire corpus. It could well be that as this technology is accepted in courtrooms and as practitioners—both producing parties and receiving parties—become familiar with it, there will be demands to expand its application because the marginal cost of doing so is minimal compared to the possible benefit of finding responsive material that would otherwise have been left behind by a culling process.[7]

An objective evaluation of TAR economics demands consideration of these factors.

## 3.8 Conclusion

In the current climate, justifying TAR relies primarily on comparison to linear review. As innovation continues to accelerate, technology-assisted review solutions will evolve. Along the way, the rationale for using TAR will likely shift from comparative review cost savings to improved quality and transparency.

There is already a trend in very large matters to evaluate quality and consistency as an integral part of the cost savings, predicated on the notion that re-performing work due to quality concerns or inconsistency will obliterate any savings achieved while prejudicing the producing party and consuming valuable time in the discovery process. In a vibrant TAR market with multiple players offering differentiated solutions, TAR is likely to become an accepted part of the discovery process, just as processing and hosting are today. As that shift happens, the evaluation of TAR will focus increasingly on distinctions between results of various approaches rather than comparisons to linear review. Doing so effectively will require parties to evaluate alternatives objectively and across multiple possible scenarios in order to choose the best option for a spectrum of possible situations.

## Notes

1. Nicholas M. Pace and Laura Zakaras, "Where the Money Goes, Understanding Litigant Expenditures for Producing Electronic Discovery," Summary ix, RAND Institute for Civil Justice (2012).
2. "EDRM Metrics Model," Budget calculators, www.edrm.net/projects/metrics/budget-calculators.
3. 11 Civ. 0691, 2013 U.S. Dist. LEXIS 36353 (S.D.N.Y. Mar. 15, 2013).
4. There will likely not be a one-to-one comparison between responsiveness precision over the entire data set and responsiveness precision over the subset of documents hit by the privilege screen.
5. "EDI-Oracle Study: Humans Are Still Essential in E-Discovery," *Law Technology News* (November 20, 2013), www.lawtechnologynews.com/id=1202628778400.

6. See Maura R. Grossman and Gordon V. Cormack, "Technology-Assisted Review in E-Discovery Can Be More Effective and More Efficient Than Exhaustive Manual Review," XVII RICH. J.L. & TECH. 11 (2011), http://jolt.richmond.edu/v17i3/article11.pdf.

7. Preculling is also under scrutiny as an obvious target of scientific validation sampling techniques developed in TAR.

# Conclusion

The impact of TAR on the evolution of electronic discovery remains to be seen. However, it would be a major loss of opportunity if the benefits of TAR were lessened because the professionals with the chance to take advantage of TAR, in representing and supporting clients in legal proceedings, did not comprehend its underpinnings sufficiently to use it appropriately and to advocate for and against its application in particular cases. This applies equally to the judiciary. It is often forgotten that the need for judges (and juries) to learn about new technology, no less so than lawyers bound by ethical obligations to do so, is not something new. Patent cases, expert reports, and other aspects of the legal system have always challenged legal professionals and the judiciary to learn new technology. The same challenge is presented by TAR.

When electronic discovery started to gain attention as a pressing threat to the legal process more than a decade ago, awareness and understanding among practitioners, as well as the judiciary, was a major factor in a constant stream of decisions issuing sanctions for malfeasance. While awareness has apparently improved dramatically, with significant efforts and resources devoted to thought leadership in the form of educational conferences and publications, sanctions continue to be issued in situations where a little learning could have prevented them. In addition, millions of dollars continue to be spent, and strategic opportunities for more successful outcomes in legal proceedings continue to be missed.

As discussed in this book, TAR has the potential to have a beneficial impact on both the unnecessary expenditure of resources and the connection between information and merits-based results in litigation. Better information, achieved more efficiently, should lead to more informed outcomes that are not based on the fact that discovery is too expensive to warrant pursuing a case, where that case otherwise should win on the merits. The transparency and economy of TAR should help the legal process work better to achieve its goals of just, speedy, and (relatively) inexpensive resolution of disputes.

TAR has been the subject of innumerable conferences and articles, but not books. This book is intended to increase understanding of TAR in a way that is in-depth and comprehensive. There may be limits to how easily meaningful knowledge about TAR can be conveyed and achieved, but such knowledge is essential to using TAR in a way that maximizes its potential.

# APPENDIX

UNITED STATES DISTRICT COURT
WESTERN DISTRICT OF LOUISIANA

| | |
|---|---|
| In Re: Actos (Pioglitazone) Products Liability Litigation | MDL NO. 6:11-md-2299 |
| | JUDGE DOHERTY |
| This Document Applies to: | MAGISTRATE JUDGE HANNA |
| All Cases | |

## CASE MANAGEMENT ORDER:
## PROTOCOL RELATING TO THE PRODUCTION OF
## ELECTRONICALLY STORED INFORMATION ("ESI")

Pursuant to the agreement reached between the Plaintiffs and Defendants herein, this Court enters the following Order concerning the production of electronically stored information in these proceedings:

**A.     Scope**

1.     General.  The procedures and protocols outlined herein govern the production of electronically stored information ("ESI") by the Parties.  Section E titled "Search Methodology Proof of Concept" applies only to the predictive coding and advanced analytics sampling procedure as outlined in that Section.  Sections A through D and Sections F through J apply throughout the pendency of this litigation.  This Order governs all parties to these proceedings, whether they currently are involved or become so in the future.  The Parties to this protocol ("Protocol") will take reasonable steps to comply with this agreed-upon Protocol for the production of documents and information existing in electronic format.  All disclosures and

{L0210836.3}

49

productions made pursuant to this Protocol are subject to the Privilege Protocol and Protective Order entered in this matter.

2.      Limitations and No-Waiver.    The Parties and their attorneys do not intend by this Protocol to waive their rights to the attorney work-product privilege, except as specifically required herein, and any such waiver shall be strictly and narrowly construed and shall not extend to other matters or information not specifically described herein. All Parties preserve their attorney client privileges and other privileges and there is no intent by the protocol, or the production of documents pursuant to the protocol, to in any way waive or weaken these privileges. All documents produced hereunder are fully protected and covered by the Parties' confidentiality agreements, and order(s) of the United States District Court, as well as any clawback agreements, and protective order(s) of the United States District Court effectuating same.

**B.      ESI Preservation**

1.      The Parties have issued litigation notices to those identified as most likely to have discoverable information.

**C.      Sources**

1.      While Defendants' fact gathering is ongoing, the following are data sources identified to date that are most likely to contain discoverable information. Defendants agree to provide additional discovered data sources likely to contain relevant information. Defendants agree to provide information about the data sources to the extent applicable and known in addition to that found in the subparagraphs below, including the date range of information contained in the data source, the department(s) utilizing the data source, whether the data source is hosted internally or externally, and the database type.

| a | ARISg | Adverse Event Database |
|---|---|---|
| b | BLUE | Labeling and promotional materials management system |
| c | Galaxy | Regulatory document management system |
| d | MEDIsource | Product information request database |
| e | T-Rx | Field sales call database |
| f | TSARS (or "S Drive") | Takeda Statistical Analysis and Repository System |
| g | T-Track | Clinical Science Liaison database |
| h | IRIS | Research grant management system |
| i | LARC | Clinical Science Liaison education resources database |
| j | Sample Guardian | Product sample management database |
| k | TEG | Takeda Educational Grant management system |
| l | PubBase | Publications management system |
| m | Records Management System | Records Operation Center ("ROC") information system |

      a.     <u>ARISg</u>: ARISg is an adverse event database. It contains information that the Pharmacovigilance department at TRGD U.S. receives regarding adverse events related to Takeda drugs, including adverse event reports ("AERs") received from, without limitation, physicians, patients, clinical trials, medical literature, and foreign entities. ARISg is the software used for this database, which is sometimes called T-Gaea within Takeda. It has been in effect since 1999.

      b.     <u>BLUE</u>: This database is used by the Marketing department in the approval process for promotional materials. It contains a labeling module and a module for promotional pieces and marketing campaigns. BLUE has been active from April 2008 to present. The vendor is Schawk Blue.

      c.     <u>Galaxy</u>: Galaxy is a document repository system used by the Regulatory department containing components of regulatory submissions to the Food and Drug Administration. It went into production in 2009.

d.  MEDIsource: This data system is used by the Medical Information and Quality Assurance departments to capture and respond to product information requests and non-medical product complaints. It has a Siebel component that documents the intake of requests for information from physicians and provides a response; a Documentum system with standard response and customer response letters; and Info Maestro which pulls information from the standard response letter and from the Sieble system to create the response letter to an individual physician.

e.  T-Rx: This database contains information regarding U.S. commercial field sales calls.

f.  TSARS (or "S Drive"): This is Takeda's Statistical Analysis and Repository System and is a Unix centralized repository used to manage Clinical and research data. It is used by the Analytical Science department. It contains clinical SAS data sets and programs used to analyze those data sets for purposes of final submission reports – tables, listings, and graphs.

g.  T-Track: This database is a customized application of Seibel's Customer Relationship Management system for use by Takeda's field based Clinical Science Liaisons.

h.  IRIS: This system is used by Takeda for the intake and processing of external research grant requests. It is a vendor hosted system (SteepRock is the vendor). It was implemented within the last five years.

i.  LARC: This database includes articles, presentations, and publications related to Takeda products and the therapeutic areas they address. Quosa is the vender for this database. It is accessible by Clinical Science Liaisons in their respective therapeutic areas.

      j.     <u>Sample Guardian</u>: This database contains product sample management data regarding sample transactions and inventory reconciliations.

      k.     <u>TEG</u>: Takeda Educational Grant database is used for education grant request management.

      l.     <u>PubBase</u>: PubBase is a Documentum-based system used for the management and storage of publication documents.

      m.     <u>Records Management System</u>: This data source is used by the Records Operations Center ("ROC"), where physical records are maintained.

**D.    Custodians**

      1.     The following are custodians who have been identified as most likely to have information relevant to this litigation. For these custodians, data is being pulled from e-mail, computer hard drives, and physical files that are in the possession, custody, and control of Takeda. Investigation is ongoing by both Parties as to potential additional custodians at Takeda (including potential Japanese custodians) and Eli Lilly and Company. Current key custodians include:

| 1. | Baron, David | Vice President, NonClinical Safety/Efficacy |
|---|---|---|
| 2. | Spanheimer, Robert | Vice President, Medical and Scientific Affairs |
| 3. | Greeby, Jennifer | Director, Marketing (Diabetes) |
| 4. | Recker, David | Senior Vice President, Clinical Science |
| 5. | Paris, Maria | Former Vice President, Pharmacovigilance |
| 6. | Gerrits, Charles | Former Senior Director, Pharmacoepidemiology |
| 7. | Johnston, Janet | Associate Director, Safety Surveillance |
| 8. | Thom, Claire | Former Vice President, Research and Development |
| 9. | Daly, Rich | Former Vice President, Marketing |
| 10. | Perez, Alfonso | Vice President, Clinical Science Strategy |

| 11. | Ortell, Una | Director, Promotion and Advertising |
| 12. | Orlando, Dan | Former Vice President, Sales |
| 13. | Lee, Jessie | Manager, Regulatory Affairs Strategy |
| 14. | Cuomo, Maryann | Associate Director, Regulatory Labeling |
| 15. | Weisbrich, Shay | Vice President, Franchise Leader (Former Director, Marketing) |
| 16. | Kupfer, Stuart | Vice President, Clinical Science |
| 17. | Ramstack, Mary | Sr. Director, Strategic Project Planning and Management |
| 18. | Roebel, Mick | Sr. Director, Regulatory Affairs |
| 19. | Lorenz, Janet | Associate Director, Regulatory Affairs, Promotion and Advertising |
| 20. | Pritza, Mary Jo | Former Associate Director, Regulatory Affairs |
| 21. | Caracci, Mike | Former Director, Marketing |
| 22. | Tynan, Julie | Assistant Project Director, Strategic Project and Planning Management |
| 23. | Hull, Andy | Vice President, Alliance Management (former Vice President, Marketing) |
| 24. | Fusco, Gregory | Sr. Medical Director, Pharmacoepidemiology and Analysis |
| 25. | Caggiano, Christopher | Sr. Product Manager, Diabetes Marketing |
| 26. | Ryan, D'Arcy | Former Director, Marketing |
| 27. | Khan, Mehmood | Former Sr. Vice President, Medical and Scientific Affairs |
| 28. | Harris, Thomas | Vice President, Regulatory Affairs |
| 29. | Trochanov, Anton | Associate Medical Director, Pharmacovigilance |

## E.   Search Methodology Proof of Concept

1.   General.   The Parties have discussed the methodologies or protocols for the search and review of ESI collected from Takeda sources, including but not limited to e-mail, and the following is a summary of the Parties' agreement on the use of a search methodology proof of concept to evaluate the potential utility of advanced analytics as a document identification mechanism for the review and production of this data.   The Parties agree to meet and confer regarding the use of advanced analytics for other data sources.   While the Parties agree to explore the use of advanced analytics as a technique to ensure appropriate responses to discovery

requests, the Parties agree that Defendants retain the right to review documents after predictive coding but prior to production for relevance, confidentiality, and privilege. A sampling of documents withheld after such review will take place pursuant to Section E.10.

    2.    General Overview of Advanced Analytics/Predictive Coding Process. Takeda utilizes software provided by Epiq Systems ("Epiq") to search and review ESI for production in this case. Epiq uses Equivio's Relevance software for advanced analytics and predictive coding.

    Epiq will collect e-mail documents from four key Takeda custodians, which will be combined to create the "sample collection population." The Parties will meet and confer to determine the names of the four custodians. Additionally, Takeda will add a set of regulatory documents which have already been collected to the "sample collection population." Takeda and Plaintiffs will each nominate three individuals ("the experts") to work collaboratively at the offices of Nelson Mullins, 1320 Main Street, Columbia, SC 29201 to train the Equivio Relevance system. Plaintiffs' experts will execute a Nondisclosure and Confidentiality Agreement in the form attached as Exhibit A hereto. To the extent that Plaintiffs' experts are exposed to information that would be subject to withholding or redaction under the Protective Order in this matter, Plaintiffs' experts agree not to disclose such information to co-counsel, client, any Party, or any third party without obtaining prior written consent of the other Party regarding the particular piece of information sought to be disclosed. Before the meeting, the Parties shall be provided a copy of the applicable Equivio training documents, handbook, or manual. The Parties' experts will receive technical training on the Equivio Relevance software and coding process and will work together to make one relevance decision for documents in the Control and Training sets, as described in more detail below.

The Parties will review a number of documents required by the Equivio Relevance system for the data to reach Stability as described below. Once Stability is reached, the Control and Training sets are then used to begin the predictive coding process. Using the Control and Training documents, the system calculates relevance scores for the entire sample collection population, with each document in the sample collection population receiving a relevance score of 0 through 100.

Attorneys representing Takeda will have access to the entire sample collection population to be searched and will lead the computer training, but they will work collaboratively with Plaintiffs' counsel during the Assessment and Training phases. Takeda's experts will conduct an initial review of documents presented by the Equivio Relevance system for privilege. The privileged documents will be either entirely withheld from viewing by Plaintiffs' experts or printed and redacted. A privilege log for such documents will be provided. The Parties, after review of the privilege log, reserve the right to require that such documents be deemed as "skip" (same as designation used for technical problem documents). Otherwise, these documents may still be used to train the system. Both Parties will then review all of the non-privileged documents during the training process (i.e., both documents coded as relevant and irrelevant). The Parties' experts will review the documents in collaboration and determine the coding to be applied to the documents. To the extent the Parties disagree regarding the coding of a particular document or designation of privilege, they will meet and confer in an effort to resolve the dispute prior to contacting the Court for resolution.

At the conclusion of the training process and upon calculation of relevance scores, the Parties will meet and confer regarding which relevance score will provide a cutoff for documents to be manually reviewed by defense counsel for production. However, the Parties reserve the right to seek relief from the Court prior to the commencement of the final manual review.

At the recommendation of Epiq, no seeding will take place at this time. The Parties may meet and confer if it is determined that seeding may be applicable at a later date.

Plaintiffs' experts and counsel shall not remove any of the Control or Training documents from the offices of Nelson Mullins, nor shall they be allowed to copy such documents. The Parties agree that Defendants do not waive protection of trade secret or confidential information in allowing Plaintiffs to review documents under this sampling mechanism. All documents reviewed pursuant to this sampling protocol shall be done under the Protective Order in this matter as well as any Privilege Protocol or clawback agreement that shall be reduced to an order acceptable to the Court.

3.     <u>Relevance Tags</u>. The Parties agree that as part of the Assessment and Training phases, all of the non-privileged and privilege-redacted documents reviewed by both parties' experts will be categorized as relevant, not relevant, or skip (to be used for documents with technical problems). The privileged-withheld documents will be categorized by Defendants' experts as relevant, not relevant, or skip, subject to the Parties' right to have any privileged-withheld documents categorized as a "skip." The Parties shall immediately discuss any disagreements on coding in good faith, so that the training may be improved accordingly, and may seek guidance from the Court or the Court appointed special masters if necessary.

4.     <u>Collection & Data Preparation</u>. The Parties will meet and confer to agree upon the four custodians that will be selected for the sampling. E-mail and attachment documents will be collected from the four custodians and added to the collected regulatory documents, together

comprising the sample collection population. Documents may be removed from the sample collection population if they are:

    a.     Spam,

    b.     Commercial e-mail,

    c.     Files without text,

    d.     Exact duplicates within the custodians (see Section G.6 regarding production of information for duplicate documents), and

    e.     System files, etc. (*i.e.*, the documents that the samples will be selected from will be de-NISTED)

Epiq will extract the sample collection population documents' text and build an index.

5.    <u>Assessment Phase</u>. The Equivio Relevance software generates an initial simple random sample of 500 documents from the sample collection population. Takeda's experts will initially review the documents for privilege. Any documents deemed privileged by Takeda's experts will be either entirely withheld from viewing by Plaintiffs' experts or printed and redacted prior to viewing by Plaintiffs' experts, and logged on a privilege log consistent with the Privilege Protocol in this matter. These documents may still be used to train the system. To the extent the Parties disagree regarding the privilege decision for a particular document, they will meet and confer in an effort to resolve the dispute prior to contacting the Court for resolution. The Parties' experts will then work collaboratively to determine the relevance of the non-privileged and privilege-redacted documents. The relevance of the privileged-withheld documents will be determined by Defendants' experts. The documents reviewed in the Assessment Phase make up the Control Set. The Control Set is used for estimating richness

(percentage of relevant documents in a population), and also serves as a reference point for calculating recall and precision.

   a.    The application's estimates of richness use a confidence level of 95%. The initial Control Set of 500 documents yields a confidence estimation of richness with an error margin of plus or minus 4.3%. This is a worst-case error margin assuming richness of 50%. For lower levels of richness, the error margin will also be lower. For example, for richness of 10%, the error margin would be plus or minus 2.6%, while for 5%, the error margin would be plus or minus 1.9%.

   b.    The Control Set also creates a basis for calculating recall and precision, which are then used for monitoring training progress and calculating results.

   c.    Equivio Relevance tracks the progress of the Assessment Phase to achieve the appropriate level of statistical validation. These levels of validation are referred to in the Equivio system as "Baseline," at the lowest level, through "Statistical," at the highest level. The terms "Baseline" and "Statistical" are used by Equivio Relevance as indicators to the user as to the progress of the Assessment Phase. The validation level achieved depends on the number of relevant documents found by the user in the Control Set. At the "Baseline" level, the number of relevant documents in the control set is too low to allow statistically valid estimates of recall and precision. The Parties will ensure that the number of Control Set documents reviewed will reach the "Statistical" level.

   d.    For informational purposes, the "Statistical" level of validation in Equivio requires the presence of at least 70 relevant documents in the Control Set. For document collections with richness of 14% and above, a Control Set of 500 documents is sufficient to reach the "Statistical" level of validation. For lower levels of richness, additional documents will need to be reviewed in the Assessment Phase in order to reach the "Statistical" level.

        e.      Based on a confidence level of 95%, the Statistical level of validation yields an error margin on recall estimates of plus or minus 11.7%. This is a worst-case error margin assuming recall of 50%. The Parties will continue the Assessment Phase, beyond the "Statistical" level, until the Control Set contains at least 385 relevant documents. This sample will yield an error margin on recall estimates of plus or minus 5%.

        6.      <u>Iterative Training Phase</u>. Following the creation of the Control Set at the Statistical validation level, the Equivio Relevance system selects a random sample of forty documents. Takeda's experts will initially review the forty documents for privilege. Any documents deemed privileged by Takeda's experts will be either entirely withheld from viewing by Plaintiffs' experts or printed and redacted prior to viewing by Plaintiffs' experts, and logged on a privilege log consistent with the Privilege Protocol in this matter. These documents may still be used to train the system. The Parties' experts will then work collaboratively to determine the relevance of the non-privileged and privilege-redacted documents. The relevance of the privileged-withheld documents will be determined by Defendants' experts, subject to the Parties' right to have any privileged-withheld documents categorized as a "skip" and not included in the training. To the extent the Parties disagree regarding the relevance or privilege decision for a particular document, they will meet and confer in an effort to resolve the dispute prior to contacting the Court for resolution.

        a.      Once the experts have completed the first Training Set, the Equivio Relevance system calculates the Training Status. The three possible states are "Not Stable," "Nearly Stable," or "Stable."

      b.      The experts continue to review samples of forty documents each, using the process outlined in paragraph 6 above, until the Stable Training Status is reached.

      c.      The subsequent samples of forty documents are selected using an Active Learning approach. Active Learning means that each training sample is selected based on what has been learned from previous samples. The object is to maximize the sample's contribution to the training process. Therefore, the system chooses samples that provide comprehensive coverage of the population (reducing under-inclusiveness), while fine-tuning the concept of relevance that the Classifier is developing (reducing over-inclusiveness). The system reaches Stability when the marginal contribution of additional samples to the enhancement of the Classifier approaches zero, as determined by the Equivio software and which determination (Stability) is not configurable.

      7.      <u>Calculation of Relevance Scores</u>. Upon completion of the Training Phase once Stability is reached, and any related meet and confer sessions and agreed upon coding corrections, the Equivio Relevance system will run over the sample collection population and calculate relevance scores for each document in the sample collection population. Each document in the sample collection population receives a relevance score of 0 through 100, with 0 being least likely to be relevant and 100 being most likely.

      8.      <u>Final Search, Review, and Production of Sample Collection Population Documents</u>. The Parties will meet and confer regarding which relevance score will provide a cutoff that will yield a proportionate set of documents that will be manually reviewed by Takeda for production. All of the documents above the agreed upon relevance score in the sample collection population will be reviewed by Takeda. Documents found by Takeda's review to be relevant and non-privileged documents will be produced to Plaintiffs.

9.      Quality Control by Random Sample of Irrelevant Documents. In addition, at the conclusion of the process described above, and prior to generating the review set, the Parties will collaboratively review at the offices of Nelson Mullins in Columbia, SC a random sample of documents in the sample collection population with relevance scores below the cut-off score set for establishing the review set (aka the "Rest"). These documents are flagged for culling, and will not be included in the review set. In Equivio Relevance, this test is referred to as "Test the Rest." The purpose for this phase is to verify that the Rest contains a low prevalence of relevant documents and that the proportionality assumptions underlying the cut-off decision are valid.

a.      The Test the Rest sample is designed to provide a confidence level of 95%. The default sample size is 500 documents. The margin of error depends on the percentage of relevant documents in the Rest. For example, if 5% of the Rest documents are found to be relevant, the margin of error is 1.9%. If 1% are relevant, the margin of error is 0.8%.

b.      Takeda's experts will initially review the Rest sample documents for privilege. Any documents deemed privileged by Takeda's experts will be either entirely withheld from viewing by Plaintiffs' experts or printed and redacted prior to viewing by Plaintiffs' experts, and logged on a privilege log consistent with the Privilege Protocol in this matter. The Parties' experts will then work collaboratively to determine the relevance of the non-privileged and privilege-redacted documents. The relevance of the privileged-withheld documents will be determined by Defendants' experts, subject to the Parties' rights to have any privilege-withheld document categorized as a "skip" for purposes of the Test the Rest sample. To the extent the Parties disagree regarding the relevance or privilege decision for a particular document, they will meet and confer in an effort to resolve the dispute prior to contacting the Court for resolution.

10. <u>Sampling of Documents Not Produced After Predictive Coding</u>. After the predictive coding process completes, and Takeda's counsel reviews and produces documents from the sample collection population consistent with paragraph 8, the Parties will collaboratively review at the offices of Nelson Mullins in Columbia, SC a random sample of documents above the agreed-upon cutoff relevance score that were withheld from production on relevance grounds. The Parties agree to meet and confer regarding an appropriate sample size.

       a.     Takeda's experts will initially review the sample documents for privilege. Any documents deemed privileged by Takeda's experts will be either entirely withheld from viewing by Plaintiffs' experts or printed and redacted prior to viewing by Plaintiffs' experts, and logged on a privilege log consistent with the Privilege Protocol in this matter. The Parties' experts will then work collaboratively to determine the relevance of the non-privileged and privilege-redacted documents. The relevance of the privileged-withheld documents will be determined by Defendants' experts, subject to the Parties' rights to have any privilege-withheld document categorized as a "skip" for this purpose. To the extent the Parties disagree regarding the relevance or privilege decision for a particular document, they will meet and confer in an effort to resolve the dispute prior to contacting the Court for resolution.

11.    <u>Post-Predictive Coding Sampling Meet and Confer</u>. The Parties shall meet and confer in good faith to resolve any difficulties and finalize the method for searching documents on a going forward basis. To the extent that the Parties cannot agree, they shall apply to the Court for relief. Defendant shall not be required to proceed with the final search and review unless and until objections raised by either Party have been adjudicated by the Court or resolved by written agreement of the Parties. The Parties reserve the right to request a meet and confer

regarding the designation of any document as a "skip" for purposes of the control sample, training, or Test the Rest, if agreement cannot be reached.

**F.    Costs**

1.    Takeda reserves its right to seek relief from the Court (e.g., a cost shifting award and pursuant to the principles of proportionality).    *See* Fed. R. Civ. P. 1, 26(b)(2)(C), 26(b)(2)(B), & 26(g); *Electronic Discovery*, 11 Sedona Conf. J. 289 (2010); *see also* Fed. R. Evid. 403 (inadmissibility of cumulative evidence).

2.    Plaintiffs agree to bear all of the costs associated with their compliance with the terms of this protocol.  Plaintiffs agree to bear all of the costs associated with the receipt and review of ESI produced hereunder including the costs associated with its ESI experts who will be involved with Plaintiffs in all aspects of this ESI protocol.

**G.    Format of Production For Documents Produced by Defendants**

1.    TIFF/Native File Format Production.  Documents will be produced as single-page TIFF images with corresponding multi-page text, native file format document if applicable under paragraph G.2, and necessary load files.  Native files, along with all corresponding metadata, will be preserved.  TIFF images will be of 300 dpi quality or better.  The load files will include an image load file as well as a metadata (.DAT) file with the metadata fields identified below on the document level to the extent available.

| | Field | Summation Field (Florida) | Definition | Doc Type |
|---|---|---|---|---|
| 1 | SOURCE | SOURCE | Name of party producing the document | All |
| 2 | CUSTODIAN | CUSTODIAN | Name of person or non-human data source from where documents/files are produced. **Where redundant names occur, individuals should be distinguished by an initial which is kept constant throughout productions (e.g., Smith, John A. and Smith, John B. Where data is collected from an archive, the archive will be listed as custodian.* | All |
| 3 | CUSTODIANAPPEN DMULTI | CUSTODIANAPPENDM ULTI | Name of Takeda person or non-human data source from where duplicate documents/files were suppressed. **Where redundant names occur, individuals should be distinguished by an initial which is kept constant throughout productions (e.g., Smith, John A. and Smith, John B. Where data is collected from an archive, the archive will be listed as custodian.* | All |
| 4 | CUSTODIAN ID | CUSTODIAN ID | Each CUSTODIAN from #2 or 3 above will be assigned a unique numeric identifier that will be maintained throughout productions. Where data is collected from an archive, the archive will be listed as custodian. | All |

| | Field | Summation Field (Florida) | Definition | Doc Type |
|---|---|---|---|---|
| 5 | BEGBATES | BEGDOC# | Beginning Bates Number (production number) | All |
| 6 | ENDBATES | ENDDOC# | End Bates Number (production number) | All |
| 7 | PGCOUNT | PGCOUNT | Number of pages in the document | All |
| 8 | FILESIZE | FILESIZE | File Size | All |
| 9 | APPLICAT | APPLICAT | Commonly associated application for the specified file type. | All |
| 10 | FILEPATH | FILEPATH (for Edocs) | File source path for electronically collected documents other than emails, which includes location, file name, and file source extension. | Edocs |
| 11 | RELATIVE PATH APPEND | RELATIVE PATH APPEND (for Edocs) | File source path for duplicate electronically collected documents other than emails, which includes location, file name, and file source extension. | Edocs |
| 12 | NATIVEFILELINK | DOCLINK | For documents provided in native format only | All |
| 13 | TEXTPATH | LOGFILE or FULLTEXT | File path for OCR or Extracted Text files | All |
| 14 | MSGID | MSGID | Value extracted from parent message during processing | Email |
| 15 | FROM | FROM | Sender | Email |
| 16 | TO | TO | Recipient | Email |
| 17 | cc | cc | Additional Recipients | Email |
| 18 | BCC | BCC | Blind Additional Recipients | Email |
| 19 | SUBJECT | SUBJECT | Subject line of email | Email |
| 20 | PARENTBATES | PARENTID | BeginBates number for the parent email of a family (will not be populated for documents that are not part of a family) | Email |

| | Field | Summation Field (Florida) | Definition | Doc Type |
|---|---|---|---|---|
| 21 | ATTACHBATES | ATTACHID | Bates number from the first page of each attachment | Email |
| 22 | BEGATTACH | (will be provided from ATTRANGE) | First Bates number of family range (i.e. Bates number of the first page of the parent email) | Email |
| 23 | ENDATTACH | (will be provided from ATTRANGE) | Last Bates number of family range (i.e. Bates number of the last page of the last attachment) | Email |
| 24 | ATTACHCOUNT | ATTACHMENT COUNT | Number of attachments to an email | Email |
| 25 | ATTACHNAME | ATTACHMENT LIST | Name of each individual attachment | Email |
| 26 | DATESENT (mm/dd/yyyy hh:mm:ss AM) | DATESENT | Date Sent | Email |
| 27 | DATERCVD (mm/dd/yyyy hh:mm:ss AM) | DATERCVD | Date Received | Email |
| 28 | EMAILDATSORT (mm/dd/yyyy hh:mm:ss AM) | DATESENT | Sent Date of the parent email (physically top email in a chain, I.e. immediate/direct parent email) | Email |
| 29 | Email Outlook Type | Email Outlook Type | Type of Outlook item, e.g.email, calendar item, contact, note, task | Email |
| 30 | HASHVALUE | MD5HASH | MD5 Hash Value | All |
| 31 | TITLE | DOCTITLE | Title provided by user within the document | Edocs |
| 32 | AUTHOR | AUTHOR | Creator of a document | Edocs |
| 33 | DATECRTD | DATECRTD | Creation Date | Edocs |
| 34 | MODIFIED BY | LAST EDITED BY | Person who has modified a document | Edocs |
| 35 | LASTMODD (mm/dd/yyyy | LASTMODD (mm/dd/yyyy hh:mm:ss | Last Modified Date | Edocs |

| | Field | Summation Field (Florida) | Definition | Doc Type |
|---|---|---|---|---|
| 36 | DocumentType | DocumentType | Descriptor for the type of document: **"E-document"** for electronic documents not attached to emails; **"Emails"** for all emails; **"E-attachments"** for files that were attachments to emails; and **"Physicals"** for hard copy physical documents that have been scanned and converted to an electronic image. | All |
| 37 | Importance | Importance | High Importance - indicates Priority Email message. | Email |
| 38 | Redacted | Redacted | Descriptor for documents that have been redacted. "Yes" for redacted documents; "No" for unredacted documents. | All |
| 39 | ProdVol | ProdVol | Name of media that data was produced on.\n\nWave 00 I - Hard Drive | All |
| 40 | Confidentiality | Confidentiality | Indicates if the document has been designated as "Confidential" pursuant to any applicable Protective Order. "Yes" for Confidential documents; **"No"** for documents that are not so designated. | All |
| 41 | Email folder | Email folder | Folder in which non-archive collected email is stored within the custodians mailbox, such as "inbox", "sent", "deleted", "draft", or any custom folder. | Email |

| | Field | Summation Field (Florida) | Definition | Doc Type |
|---|---|---|---|---|
| 42 | Relevance score | Relevance score | Relevance score assigned by Equivio for documents that have been through the predictive coding process | All |

     a.     This list of fields does not create any obligation to create or manually code fields that are not automatically generated by the processing of the ESI; that do not exist as part of the original Metadata of the document; or that would be burdensome or costly to obtain.

     2.     Defendants will produce spreadsheets (.xls/.xlsx files) and PowerPoint presentations (.ppt/.pptx files) in native form as well as audio and video files (e.g., mp3s, wavs, mpegs, etc.), except that spreadsheets and PowerPoint documents will be produced in TIFF format if redactions are applied. Audio and video files shall be edited if redactions are required, subject to appropriate identification of any such audio or video files having been edited. In addition, for any redacted documents that are produced, the documents' metadata fields will be redacted where required. The Parties will meet and confer regarding a request for the production of any other materials including documents in native file format.

     3.     The Parties agree to meet and confer regarding the format of production for structured databases.

     4.     <u>Appearance</u>. Subject to appropriate redaction, each document's electronic image will convey the same information and image as the original document, including formatting, such as bolding, highlighting, font size, italics. Documents will be produced in black and

white.  After production, a Party may request that a document be produced in color at which time the Parties may meet and confer about such production.  Documents that present imaging or formatting problems will be identified and the Parties will meet and confer in an attempt to resolve the problems.

5.  Document Numbering.  Each page of a produced document will have a legible, unique page identifier "Bates Number" electronically "burned" onto the image at a location that does not obliterate, conceal or interfere with any information from the source document.  The Bates Number for each page of each document will be created so as to identify the producing Party and the document number.  In the case of materials redacted in accordance with applicable law or confidential materials contemplated in any Protective Order or Confidentiality Stipulation entered into by the Parties, a designation may be "burned" onto the document's image at a location that does not obliterate or obscure any information from the source document.

6.  De-NISTing and Deduplication.  Electronic file collections will be De-NISTed, removing commercially available operating system and application file contained on the current NIST file list.  Defendants will globally deduplicate identical ESI as follows:

a.  Electronic Files:  Duplicated electronic files will be identified based upon calculated MD5 Hash values for binary file content. File contents only will be used for MD5 Hash value calculation and will not include operating system metadata (filename, file dates) values. All files bearing an identical MD5 hash value are a duplicate group.  The document reviewed by Defendants for privilege, relevance, or confidentiality shall be deemed the primary duplicate document within the group.  Generally, the Defendants shall not remove any of the objective coding fields listed in paragraph G.1 above, in either primary or duplicate documents. If redactions are applied to the subject and/or text fields, however, Defendants may apply the same redactions to all other documents within the duplicate group.  Defendants shall only produce one document image or native file for duplicate ESI documents within the group.  For Takeda sources, the following metadata fields as described in Section G.1 associated with the produced document will provide information for duplicate documents not produced: CustodianAppendMulti and RelativePathAppend.

      b.    Messaging Files: Duplicate messaging files will be identified based upon MD5 Hash values for the message family, including parent object and attachments. The following fields will be used to create the unique value for each message:  To; From; CC; BCC; Date Sent; Subject; Body; and, MD5 Hash values for all attachments, in attachment order. Duplicate messaging materials will be identified at a family level, including message and attachment(s).  All files bearing an identical MD5 Hash value are a duplicate group.  The documents reviewed by Defendants for privilege, relevance, or confidentiality shall be deemed the primary duplicate document within the group.  For identified duplicate ESI, the Defendants shall not remove any of the objective coding fields listed in paragraph G.1 above.  If redactions have been applied to such fields, Defendants may substitute and replace the subject and text fields with those reviewed by Defendants' counsel for the primary duplicate ESI document for the other documents within the duplicate group.  Defendants shall only produce one document image or native file for duplicate ESI documents within the group.  For Takeda sources, the following metadata field as described in Section G.1 associated with the produced document will provide information for duplicate documents not produced: CustodianAppendMulti.

      c.    E-mail Threading:  The producing Party may identify e-mail threads where all previous emails which make up the thread are present in the body of the final e-mail in the thread.  Any party electing to use this procedure must notify all receiving parties that e-mail thread suppression has been proposed to be performed on a specified production and the Parties agree to meet and confer regarding the format of this production, and reserve the right to seek Court guidance on the issue should agreement not be reached.

7.   Production Media.  The producing Party may produce documents via a secure file transfer mechanism and/or on readily accessible, computer or electronic media as the Parties may hereafter agree upon, including CD-ROM, DVD, external hard drive (with standard PC compatible interface), (the "Production Media").  Each piece of Production Media will be assigned a production number or other unique identifying label corresponding to the date of the production of documents on the Production Media (e.g., "Defendant Takeda Production April 1, 2012") as well as the sequence of the material in that production (e.g. "-001", "-002").  For example, if the production comprises document images on three DVDs, the producing Party may label each DVD in the following manner "Defendant Takeda Production April 1, 2012", "Defendant MSL Production April 1, 2012-002", "Defendant Takeda Production April 1, 2012-003."  Additional information that will be identified on the physical Production Media includes: (1) text referencing that it was produced in *In re: Actos (Pioglitazone) Products Liability Litigation;* and (2) the Bates Number range of the materials contained on the Production Media.  Further, any replacement Production Media will cross-reference the original Production Media and clearly identify that it is a replacement and cross-reference the Bates Number range that is being replaced.

8.   Write Protection and Preservation.  All computer media that is capable of write protection should be write-protected before production.

9.   Inadvertent Disclosures.  The terms of the Case Management Order: Assertions of Attorney-Client Privilege and Work Product Doctrine shall apply to this protocol.

10. <u>Duplicate Production Not Required</u>. The Parties shall meet and confer regarding any Party's request to produce identical paper copies of data already produced in electronic form.

**H.** **Timing.**

1. The Parties will use their reasonable efforts to produce ESI in a timely manner consistent with the Court's discovery schedule.

2. The Parties will produce ESI on a rolling basis.

**I.** **General Provisions.**

1. Any practice or procedure set forth herein may be varied by agreement of the Parties, and first will be confirmed in writing, where such variance is deemed appropriate to facilitate the timely and economical exchange of electronic data.

2. Should any Party subsequently determine it cannot in good faith proceed as required by this protocol; the Parties will meet and confer to resolve any dispute before seeking Court intervention.

3. The Parties agree that e-discovery will be conducted in phases and the Parties will meet and confer regarding discovery of data sources not listed herein.

4. Regardless of the foregoing, the Parties are under a continuing obligation to produce identified responsive, non-privileged documents and to identify sources of potentially discoverable materials consistent with their obligations under Federal Rules of Civil Procedure.

**J.** **Items Requiring Meet and Confer**.

1. The Parties agree to meet and confer regarding the following items in advance of impacted productions:

     a. Whether the E-mail Property metadata field is able to be produced

     b. Certain technical specifications for productions:

(1) Hard copy document unitization

(2) Microsoft "Auto" features or macros

(3) Embedded objects

(4) Compressed Files

(5) Load file organization

**IT IS SO ORDERED.**

THUS DONE AND SIGNED in Lafayette, Louisiana, this _27_ day of July, 2012.

HONORABLE REBECCA F. DOHERTY
UNITED STATES DISTRICT JUDGE

# About the Contributors

**Dick Oehrle** is the chief linguist of Ernst & Young LLP's Fraud Investigation & Dispute Services practice. He specializes in the application of linguistic and statistical methods to the search, categorization, and analysis of large electronic datasets. Dr. Oehrle has led electronic discovery projects involving diverse industries (chemicals, software, telecom, pharmaceuticals, financial services), as well as investigations of electronic data related to financial fraud and stock option backdating. He has designed and implemented a variety of systems to enhance the quality of categorization and the insight of analysis, involving grammatical infrastructure for English, French, and German search support; detection and analysis of emotional expression; boilerplate privilege disclaimer isolation; rapid prototyping of complex searches; and machine-learning classifiers. He has been a leading advocate for the introduction of quantitative measures of eDiscovery quality.

Prior to joining Ernst & Young LLP, Dr. Oehrle was the chief linguist at Cataphora Legal, and a linguistics professor at Stanford and the University of Arizona. He is a past president of the Mathematics of Language Special Interest Group of the Association of Computational Linguistics and is currently serving a term on the National Conference of Lawyers and Scientists, a joint committee of the American Association for the Advancement of Science and the American Bar Association.

**Eric Johnson** is an executive director of Ernst & Young LLP's Fraud Investigation & Dispute Services practice. Focusing on eDiscovery, technology-assisted review, data analytics, and forensic technology, Mr. Johnson leads teams of engineers, computational linguists, statisticians, and IT and electronic discovery professionals. Responsible for technology-assisted review development and integrated deployment, Mr. Johnson is a 25-year legal and technology veteran whose experience includes developing and managing technically innovative electronic discovery and analytics programs. Mr. Johnson spearheads projects involving accelerated schedules and very high volumes of electronically stored information where machine learning, analytical frameworks, and computational linguistics play large roles, including big data sources such as social network media and internal corporate records. Mr. Johnson has extensive hands-on experience in matters involving intellectual property, life sciences, technology, HSR second requests, antitrust, contracts and licensing, securities, environmental, insurance, and criminal.

Prior to joining EY, Mr. Johnson spent six years as vice president of technical operations at Cataphora Legal. Before that, he spent 17 years in AmLaw 50 firms, and served as director of eDiscovery at a boutique IP firm in Silicon Valley.

**Adam Cohen** is a principal in Ernst & Young LLP's Fraud Investigation & Dispute Services practice. He has more than 15 years of experience in law and technology, and routinely advises some of the world's leading businesses on data management and electronic discovery compliance issues. Mr. Cohen's client engagements focus on large-scale investigations and litigations as well as proactive information management policies, procedures, and technology. He is a well-known author and lecturer in the field of electronic discovery, and has served as a court-appointed expert on electronic discovery issues in federal court.

Prior to his career in consulting, Mr. Cohen was a litigation partner in the New York office of Weil, Gotshal & Manges LLP, where he represented large corporate clients in complex litigation involving computer- and Internet-related issues. He is the author of *Social Media Legal Risk and Corporate Policy* (2013) and coauthor of the treatise *Electronic Discovery: Law and Practice* (2nd ed., 2013), in its eleventh year of publication. It has been cited as authority in several landmark Federal Court opinions involving electronic discovery.

Mr. Cohen is also coauthor of the *ESI Handbook: Sources, Technology, and Process* (2009) and the primary author of the New York State Bar Association's "Best Practices in eDiscovery in New York State and Federal Courts," as well as many articles in national legal and technology publications.

He serves on the advisory board of Georgetown Law School's Advanced eDiscovery Institute and has lectured at Harvard Law School. Mr. Cohen is also a member of the Sedona Conference working group on electronic discovery and has chaired the New York State Bar Association's electronic discovery committee since its inception 10 years ago.

**Jonathan Nystrom** is an executive director of Ernst & Young LLP's Fraud Investigation & Dispute Services practice. He is a key professional in the firm's Forensic Technology & Discovery Services practice, which focuses on technology-assisted review and behavioral analytics. He focuses on measurement and quality imperatives that affect defensibility and acceptance of technology in a legal context. Mr. Nystrom has more than 20 years' experience working with corporations and their counsel to address discovery and information management issues related to finding key information and interpreting it in context. He has led projects using a wide variety of technologies and protocols. Mr. Nystrom collaborates with accounting and legal professionals to develop and implement fact-finding and discovery strategies that leverage innovative technology in complex investigation and litigation matters. He was an early proponent of leveraging advanced information retrieval science in legal discovery, and has consistently pioneered new and improved applications of technology to help practitioners harvest, interpret, and manage complex information stores.

Prior to joining Ernst & Young LLP, Mr. Nystrom founded Cataphora Legal, an innovation leader in the field of legal technology services. Mr. Nystrom directed Cataphora Legal for nine years. Prior to that, Mr. Nystrom held increasingly responsible positions in the legal technology services since his start at document imaging and mass storage pioneer Intrafed, Inc. Cataphora Legal joined EY in 2011.

**Russell Miller** is a senior manager in Ernst & Young LLP's Fraud Investigation & Dispute Services practice. He has 15 years of hands-on experience integrating law and technology. He focuses on data collection, processing, and native and hard copy document review, with a focus on how to leverage technology to create cost-effective and defensible workflows. Through carefully crafted protocols and tested legal project management techniques, Mr. Miller helps clients avoid risk, reduce costs, and meet deadlines in complex litigation, antitrust, and investigative matters.

Before joining Ernst & Young LLP's Forensic Technology & Discovery Services group, Mr. Miller was a senior vice president for a leading discovery solutions provider responsible for the growth and development of managed document review services. Prior to that, Mr. Miller spent 10 years working as a litigation support specialist and consultant for a top AmLaw firm, working closely with attorneys and corporate legal departments to develop discovery strategies for the collection, processing, review, and production of electronically stored information.

# Index